# Keto Soup Cookbook

# KETO Soup COOKBOOK

## Comforting Low-Carb Favorites

Jennifer Allen

ROCKRIDGE PRESS

For general information on our other products and services or to obtain technical support, please contact our Customer Care Department within the United States at (866) 744-2665, or outside the United States at (510) 253-0500.

Rockridge Press publishes its books in a variety of electronic and print formats. Some content that appears in print may not be available in electronic books, and vice versa.

TRADEMARKS: Rockridge Press and the Rockridge Press logo are trademarks or registered trademarks of Callisto Media Inc. and/or its affiliates, in the United States and other countries, and may not be used without written permission. All other trademarks are the property of their respective owners. Rockridge Press is not associated with any product or vendor mentioned in this book.

Interior and Cover Designer: Darren Samuel
Art Producer: Samantha Ulban
Editor: Rachelle Mahoney
Production Editor: Andrew Yackira
Production Manager: Holly Haydash

Photography © 2021 Andrew Purcell, Cover; pp.112; Darren Muir, pp. ii, vi, 24, 82; Hélène Dujardin, pp. 42; Thomas J. Story, pp. x; Laura Flippen, pp. 62; Emulsion Studio, pp. 81, 98. Food Styling by Carrie Purcell, Cover.

Paperback ISBN: 978-1-63807-111-2
eBook ISBN: 978-1-63807-162-4
R0

To Matthew, Kegan, and Brenna—my biggest supporters and the best recipe testers on the planet!

# CONTENTS

# INTRODUCTION

Soup is present in some of my earliest childhood memories. I remember my parents making pots of chicken soup from rich, hearty broths made with bones that would slowly simmer. Leftover vegetables, noodles, potatoes, and anything in the refrigerator was fair game for soup ingredients. I'd come in from the cold and smell the savory aromas of soup on the stove and know that a bowlful of goodness was waiting to warm me up.

Soup is on the menu of just about every restaurant across the United States, from humble coffee shops to the fanciest restaurants. Growing up in the North, I got used to eating soups all year long.

I had a culture shock when I moved to Texas 20 years ago. Soup wasn't omnipresent in Texas restaurants the way it was where I grew up, and the available selection of canned soups in the grocery stores was dismal. I remember being sad when I realized that soups would no longer be a part of my regular meals.

When I started my career as a professional chef working in private homes, I was excited to show clients my vast repertoire of delicious soups, but nobody in Texas wanted to eat soup when it was 100 degrees outside. It wasn't until I opened my brick-and-mortar store that I could really focus on making amazing soups. The business was part deli and part gourmet-to-go, where busy customers could find scrumptious, premade frozen foods to heat at home. In addition to a daily fresh soup, I had dozens of frozen soups ready for purchase.

Of course, years working as a chef took their toll. By the time I had my second child, my weight was out of control. I had gestational diabetes with both kids and was eventually diagnosed with type 2 diabetes. I was on medications for all sorts of things, mostly related to my unhealthy lifestyle. It wasn't until after I'd sold my business and shifted my career to writing and recipe development that I felt I had the time and resources to focus on my health. I had made recipes for every kind of diet out there, so I was very familiar with keto. However, it took a real mindset shift to finally give up the carbs and switch to what has been a lifesaving way of eating. Thanks to keto, I've lost weight, my medications are reduced, and I'm on track to reverse my type 2 diabetes.

I still love soups, but now I make sure they're keto compatible by replacing carb-heavy ingredients with nutrient-dense vegetables. I love playing with flavors and textures to create amazing bowlfuls of goodness, and my freezer is always stocked with frozen keto soups. Whether it is my whole meal or just a part of it, a good soup always puts a smile on my face. I'm hoping the soups in this book do the same for you. Whether you're an experienced cook or a novice in the kitchen, the soup recipes in this book are designed to be easy, delicious, and, most important, keto. Plus, there are all types of soups in this book, including creamy, chunky, and brothy. So, grab a spoon and get ready to scoop into one of these delightful and creative recipes the next time you're craving a warm bowl of comfort.

# 1

# Making Soup Keto

Years ago, when I had my deli, a customer told me soup was nothing more than a broth of some kind with added veggies, protein, and potatoes, rice, or noodles. While this might be a broad definition of soup, there's so much more to creating wholesome, delicious, and mouthwatering soups. Making them keto is a whole other challenge. Some soups are easy to adapt to keto: just omit the carb-heavy vegetables and skip the noodles. However, the really good soups take a bit more care. Don't worry! I'm here to walk you through the process. Before you know it, you'll be digging into simple and scratch-made soups that are full of wholesome goodness.

# Soup, but Make It Keto

Soup evokes feelings of warmth and comfort, and wrapping your hands around a hot mug or bowl of soup is the ideal pick-me-up on a cold day. For many of us, soup is the perfect comfort food. However, finding a good premade keto soup can be a challenge.

The soup aisle in your grocery store is filled with a dazzling selection of soups, but even those we think might be keto can be loaded with thickeners and ingredients that can increase the carb count. Cream soups are often thickened with modified cornstarch, wheat flour, or potato starch. You'll even find these thickeners in broth-based soups, upping the carb count in each serving. Sugar is also hidden in many prepared soups. Often it's not even called "sugar," but it's still there in the form of fructose, glucose, corn syrup, or dextrose, to name a few. Always read the ingredient label and watch for hidden sugars and starches.

More keto-friendly soups are coming to your grocery store shelves all the time, but we still must be vigilant and read the nutrition labels. The lack of label regulations around keto means that many products are labeled keto (and priced accordingly) without actually being keto. While we might all know that rice and pasta are a no-no, being familiar with the names of hidden carbs and starches will help you make wise choices. Some hidden carb additives to watch out for are the following:

> **Maltodextrin**—a refined sugar

> **Agave**—a natural sugar

> **Sucrose**—a natural sugar

> **Tapioca**—a thickening agent

> **Grain**-based flours—wheat, oat, barley

> **Other flours**—rice, potato, chickpea

In this book, I've recreated soups so that you can enjoy big, bold, and exciting flavors at home without having to worry about the carbs. From homey, soul-satisfyingly chunky bowls of goodness to more refined flavors that are worthy of dinner parties, there's a variety of soups in this book to try. Each is made from wholesome keto-friendly and commonly found ingredients, and you don't need to be a professional chef to make them. From childhood favorites to new twists on old classics, you'll have no trouble finding something amazing to try.

## THE KETO DIET IN BRIEF

Our bodies are designed to burn glucose for fuel. When we eat bread, rice, pasta, or sugar (to name a few of the carb-heavy culprits), our bodies turn them into glucose. If we overeat and ingest too many carbohydrates, our insulin, a hormone created by the pancreas, will work hard to store the excess glucose as fat.

The keto (short for "ketogenic") diet has been around for decades. It was first created to help control seizures in patients with epilepsy. Emerging scientific studies have shown that limiting one's intake of carbohydrates can also have a positive effect on controlling blood sugar, inflammation, and even weight.

Ketosis is the metabolic state in which the body burns fat for fuel instead of glucose. Achieving a state of ketosis is the primary goal of a keto diet and the mechanism by which weight loss occurs.

By modifying our diets and eliminating carb-heavy foods such as breads and pastas and staying away from fruits and some vegetables, we can lower our carbohydrate consumption, thus forcing our bodies into ketosis. Most people aim for a daily maximum of 50 carbohydrates, but most keto dieters use net carbs as a measure. Net carbs are calculated by subtracting fiber and sugar alcohols from the total carbohydrates

(carbohydrates – fiber + sugar alcohols = net carbs). Among keto dieters, 20 net carbs is the magic number for achieving and staying in ketosis.

Just remember that this is a personal journey. While it might take one person a day or two to achieve ketosis, it can take another person several days or even up to a week. Also, always be sure to check with your doctor before embarking on a new diet.

## CARBS AND OTHER MACROS

The keto diet, also called a low-carb, high-fat diet, has several variations. However, for the purposes of this book and the recipes to come, we are assuming a standard keto diet that includes carefully controlled macros.

Macros are the percentage of fat, protein, and carbs in your diet. Most standard keto dieters aim for about 70 percent of their calories to come from fat, about 20 percent from protein, and about 10 percent from carbs. The actual target number of calories is based on various factors, including if you want to lose weight or are maintaining your weight. Your sex, age, height, starting weight, and activity level are also used to calculate those exact numbers. The best way to figure out your ideal macros is to use an online calculator and to remember to recalculate your macros after losing weight or changing your activity level.

To help make things easier, each of the recipes in this book contains macro breakdowns in addition to the net carb count (calculated by subtracting the fiber and sugar alcohols from the total carbs) so that you can adjust your daily meal plan. Remember that every meal doesn't have to perfectly fit into your overall macros. This means that you can indulge with something a bit higher in net carbs and compensate by keeping the carbs low across your meals for the rest of the day. Fasting is another tool used by keto dieters to regulate their daily consumption of food, allowing them to enjoy meals that are higher in carbs because they're skipping another meal. As long as you hit or get close to your target macros and net carbs each day, you should see keto success.

Most standard keto dieters aim for between 20 and 50 net carbs per day. Your total number of net carbs is a personal choice, and the recipes in this book will easily fit into your meal plan for the day. Scientifically, the human body should achieve ketosis if you consume less than 50 net carbs per day, but that number can vary from person to person. Experimenting is important, as is adjusting as you go. You should be able to sustain this way of eating and never feel deprived.

To keep the net carb count down, each of these recipes is crafted from lower-carb ingredients. I've made them robust and delicious with the use of herbs, spices, and plenty of tasty proteins. I've also included recipes with keto pasta alternatives so that you can indulge in all your favorite soups. In addition, you'll find a variety of classic soups with tasty twists, along with some of my personal favorites that I've never shared before. Thick, brothy, chunky, and creamy, there are all sorts of soups to come. Some are quick fixes, and others are labors of love. The bottom line is that if you're a soup lover, there are plenty of tasty picks in this book to inspire you.

# Soup Essentials

I was born with a whisk in one hand and a spoon in the other. In other words, I've been cooking my whole life. For a large chunk of that time, I was cooking professionally for my own businesses. I've also taught dozens of people how to cook, so no matter if you're new to keto, new to cooking, or both, I'm going to help set you up for success.

Soups are an easy way to add flavor to your day. They're nutritious and delicious, and with so many recipes to pick from, you can make a different one every time and never get tired of them. Plus, many of these soups freeze well, so they're perfect if you're batch cooking or meal prepping. And, perhaps the best part, once you've had a taste of home-cooked soup, you'll never want to go back to ultra-processed and prepared soups.

I challenge you to try something new. Flip through the recipes in this book, and if something catches your attention, make it. The recipes are easy and come with step-by-step instructions. Made with common ingredients and without fancy equipment, these soups will make you a star in your own kitchen in no time. And I'm here to help. I'm going to lay it all out for you, including the equipment you need, swaps you can make to keep things keto, and how to stock a keto pantry. I'll show you all my tips and tricks for making keto soups perfectly every time.

## WHOLE FOODS AND HIGH-QUALITY INGREDIENTS

People choose to do keto for many reasons, including losing weight, regulating blood sugar, controlling type 2 diabetes, reducing inflammation, and improving overall health. One way to achieve any of these goals is by eating wholesome, scratch-made food. Skipping processed foods and making your own meals instead of getting takeout or eating out is ultimately better for you and less expensive.

It all starts with whole foods and high-quality ingredients. Many keto dieters choose to eat organic vegetables and meats, to eat dairy from pasture-raised cows, and to only buy wild-caught and sustainable seafood. You can still achieve ketosis by choosing generic store brands rather than organic and luxe brands, and the recipes in this book are made with unprocessed and commonly available ingredients. This means that you can indulge in your favorite soup for lunch or dinner any day of the week.

To keep things simple, some of these recipes use convenience foods like canned whole tomatoes, shirataki noodles, and a variety of cheeses. Don't feel guilty about taking some shortcuts: making a delicious and wholesome keto meal is so much more important than falling back on old habits and eating carb-heavy dishes.

That said, remember to look at the ingredient labels. Canned tomatoes often have sugar in them, sausage can have hidden starchy fillers, and some chicken is injected with a brine that contains salt and starches—skip those brands. Always scan the labels to look for these hidden carbs. The good news is that once you know which brands are keto-friendly, you can buy those items again and again without having to look at the labels.

Good food starts with good ingredients. Just because you're making soup doesn't mean you should sacrifice quality.

## STOCK UP

One of my favorite tips for keto cooking is to stock up on ingredients so that you always have what you need to make something delicious. The following are some other tips to help you get ready for keto cooking success.

> **Buy in bulk.** If you have room to store ingredients, such as in the pantry or freezer, buying in bulk will ensure that you almost always have what you need to make recipes. Whether meats, cheeses, or canned goods, I always buy in bulk.

> **Shop the sales.** People are often afraid that keto is more expensive than conventional eating. However, if you shop the sales, it can actually be more affordable. Need chicken to make Chicken and Chipotle Chowder (page 76)? Don't run out to buy just one or two chicken breasts. Buy chicken on sale and freeze portions of it to use in recipes. Also, keep an eye on store flyers so that you can use price matching if your store allows it.

> **Seasonality is key.** Fresh produce is almost always cheaper (and of better quality) when it's local and in season. However, buying frozen is a smart alternative to make sure you have everything on hand to make a yummy soup. With today's technology,

frozen vegetables are as nutritious as fresh vegetables, and they'll last longer in your freezer.

› **Get rid of temptations.** Donate processed canned goods and non-keto ingredients to a charity and stock your refrigerator, freezer, and pantry with keto-friendly ingredients.

› **Utilize the rotisserie chicken.** I buy whole rotisserie chickens and pull off the meat. The bones go into a plastic bag for Chicken Bone Broth (page 26), and the meat is added to soups and stews throughout the week.

› **Purchase IQF meats.** IQF stands for "individually quickly frozen." I buy IQF chicken, fish fillets, shrimp, scallops, and more because you can take out one chicken breast, a handful of shrimp, or whatever you need without having to use the whole package. Proteins sold this way can be a bit pricier upfront, but the convenience can be worth it.

Now let's get into some specifics on what you can have on hand so that you're always ready to make something fabulous. The following list isn't exhaustive, but it'll get you started. Everything should be easy to find in your local grocery store.

## Keto Swaps

The list of high-carb ingredients found in soups is nearly endless. However, you can make your favorite soups more carb friendly with a few swaps.

Instead of pasta, use . . .

› **Shirataki noodles:** Shirataki noodles are made from a type of fiber called glucomannan, which comes from the root of a konjac plant. Sold under a variety of brand names, these noodles are very high in water and fiber, are low in calories, and contain no digestible carbs. This makes them perfect for a keto diet.

› **Spaghetti squash:** Delicate in flavor and with a hint of sweetness, cooked spaghetti squash can even be added to soups to stand in for traditional pasta.

- **Zucchini noodles:** Zucchini is available year-round in the grocery store. Buy them fresh and spiralize them yourself to make long, thin noodles (also called "zoodles"). You can also use a handheld julienne peeler to make long, thin strands. Just make sure you don't overcook the zucchini, or it'll disintegrate or get mushy.

Instead of rice, use . . .

- **Cauliflower rice:** This is a common and easy-to-make substitute. Add it near the end of the cooking time and simmer it for about two minutes. You can buy cauliflower rice frozen or fresh or you can make it yourself by pulsing cauliflower florets in your food processor until crumbly.

Instead of flour, use . . .

- **Xanthan gum:** Flour is often used in creamy soups and chowders to thicken them. I use xanthan gum instead to thicken all my soups and sauces for zero net carbs. Be very careful with xanthan gum because a little goes a long way. Start with about ¼ teaspoon of xanthan gum for at least two cups of soup. Whisk it in and let it sit to thicken. It'll thicken more as it sits, so resist the temptation to add more right away because too much will result in a slimy texture. Xanthan gum has no flavor, so it won't affect the taste of your soup.

Instead of potatoes, use . . .

- **Non-starchy vegetables:** Add turnips, kohlrabi, or even cauliflower chunks to your soup instead of carb-heavy potatoes. They won't add much flavor, but you can still have satisfying chunks in your soup without the carbs.

Instead of corn, use...

> **Sunflower seeds:** Try adding a small handful of shelled sunflower seeds. They soften up a little in the soup and provide a lovely texture without altering the flavor.

## Pantry and Spices

Stocking your pantry with essentials, including spices, is an easy way to set yourself up for keto success. Freshness and quality count with these pantry staples, too. For example, avocado oil and olive oil should be kept in dark, cool cupboards when not in use, and even dried spices lose flavor over time.

Many dried spices are available in their own grinders, and I love these. Whole spices retain their flavor much longer, and you can get freshly ground flavor at your fingertips. In addition to salt and pepper grinders, I've seen grinder jars of Italian seasoning and other spice blends, oregano, parsley, garlic, and more.

The following is a list of some must-have pantry ingredients and spices so that when you go to make your favorite soup, you're set up with the basics.

> **Avocado or olive oil:** Avocado oil is a popular choice on keto because it has a high smoking point and is an excellent oil in both hot and cold applications. Olive oil is another good choice, but if you're sautéing or frying, opt for avocado. I have both in my pantry. The soups in this cookbook will work with either avocado or olive oil, so feel free to experiment with both.

> **Black and white pepper:** Pepper is as necessary to cooking as salt, and having both black and white peppercorns in grinders is essential. Black peppercorns have a spicier kick, while white peppercorns have a milder, nuttier flavor. But the big difference is in

your soup: white pepper can be used in cream-based soups so that you don't have big, black flecks of pepper in it, and the milder flavor of the white pepper won't overwhelm your soup. Try using white pepper in place of black pepper in any cream-based soups in this book.

> **Chipotle powder:** With a lovely smoky flavor and plenty of kick, a good-quality chipotle powder will rescue many boring and bland meals.

> **Garlic powder:** There's no doubt that garlic adds a punch of flavor to recipes, but whole garlic is also higher in carbs. When you're looking for just a wee bit of garlic flavor, opt for garlic powder instead and save yourself a carb or two.

> **Himalayan pink salt:** Loaded with significantly more minerals than regular salt, Himalayan pink salt is less processed than regular table salt. Shockingly, some brands of salt add sugar in one form or another. Iodized salt contains potassium iodide, and sugar is added to prevent the potassium iodide from breaking down.

> **Italian seasoning:** A good jar of Italian seasoning is a must-have. Read the label to make sure it is free from added sugar. You can use it on nearly anything, including soups, stews, chicken, eggs, and vegetables.

## Canned and Frozen Foods

Most people don't have hours to cook a meal, and there's nothing wrong with turning to some convenience items when cooking from scratch. The following are some of my must-have canned and frozen items.

> **Bacon, frozen:** I buy ends and pieces and freeze them in ½-cup portions in zip-top bags. You can sometimes find the ends and pieces in a big bag at the grocery store, or you can stop by your favorite butcher and ask for them. Not only are they cheaper, but they'll also add plenty of meatiness to your recipes.

- **Broth, low-sodium chicken/beef:** Making your own bone broth is the way to go, but if you're out or don't have time to make more, use a good-quality boxed broth instead. Just check the ingredients, because some of those broths are loaded with artificial color, sugars, and other additives you don't want. Always go for low-sodium or even no-salt-added versions so that you can control the sodium levels of your soups. Using boxed broth is a whole lot faster than making it from scratch.

- **Cauliflower, frozen, riced:** Sometimes I make fresh riced cauliflower from scratch as a side dish, but when I want to add just a handful to a recipe, having it frozen saves plenty of time. Just take out what you need, thaw it, and add it to your recipe.

- **Sausage, frozen:** Sausage adds oodles of flavor to soups, but you probably don't need a whole package. Freeze those sausages. They break apart easily, so you can just grab one when you need it.

- **Spinach, frozen:** Buy the kind that comes in little pucks or cubes so that you can take out as much as you need and keep the rest frozen for another recipe. Just remember to thaw and squeeze it well before adding it to any soups or stews or else you'll dilute the broth.

- **Tomatoes, canned:** Tomatoes are incredibly perishable. While fresh tomatoes add a lovely flavor to recipes, canned tomatoes will do just fine in most dishes, and you can't beat the convenience. Look for brands without any added sugar and keep a variety of canned tomatoes on hand, including diced, whole, and crushed. Fire-roasted tomatoes are another great pick.

- **Tuna, salmon, chicken, and ham, canned:** Need protein in a hurry? Get great-quality tuna, salmon, chicken, and even ham in portion-controlled cans. They are perfect in soups, because you can add as much as needed without cooking the protein from scratch.

## Fresh Vegetables

Keto isn't all about bacon and cream. Vegetables are important, too. By eating a variety of vegetables, and even trying some new ones, you can add color, texture, nutrients, and flavor to your meals. I almost always recommend using fresh vegetables over frozen because they generally are superior in flavor and texture. While you can find many vegetables frozen, there are some that you should absolutely eat fresh if possible. I'll break it down for you.

**Best when fresh:** Onions, garlic, cabbage, Brussels sprouts, zucchini, bell peppers, celery

**Suitable when frozen:** Spinach, green beans, carrots, cauliflower, broccoli, kale

If you're stocking your refrigerator with keto vegetables or you're just getting ready for a shop, the following keto-friendly vegetables are great to have on hand. They keep well in the refrigerator and are best when eaten fresh.

- **Cabbage:** Green and red cabbage will keep in the refrigerator for weeks.
- **Carrots:** Carrots are higher in carbs, but you need just a few to add plenty of flavor, color, and crunch.
- **Garlic:** Fresh garlic is far superior in flavor to jarred minced garlic.
- **Onions:** Opt for yellow and red onions, as sweet onions are higher in carbs.
- **Shallots:** Onion's milder cousin, shallots are root vegetables with a subtle onion-garlic flavor. I use them instead of onions in milder-flavored recipes, but they're perfect in just about anything.
- **Turnips:** Perfect for mashing or adding to soups and stews, turnips are lowish-carb root vegetables that keep for a few weeks in the crisper drawer of the refrigerator.

## Meat, Fish, and Poultry

There are many types of protein you can enjoy on a keto diet, such as beef, pork, poultry, and a variety of seafood. It can make grocery shopping confusing and overwhelming. To get you started, here's a list of keto-friendly meats and seafood to consider purchasing.

‣ **Beef:** ground beef, steaks (New York strip, ribeye, sirloin, etc.), roasts (rib roast, eye of round, chuck roast, etc.), stew beef, beef ribs, beef tenderloin

‣ **Chicken:** ground chicken, chicken breast, chicken legs, chicken thighs

‣ **Pork:** ground pork, pork tenderloin, pork ribs, sausage (read the ingredient labels for hidden carbs), bacon

‣ **Seafood:** most salt and freshwater fish, shrimp, canned tuna, lobster (Mussels, oysters, and octopus are a bit higher in carbs, so eat those in moderation.)

Now that you know what to buy, here are some tips to help you navigate the meat and seafood sections of your supermarket.

1. **Buy what you can afford.** Grass-fed, organic, and other labels often come with a hefty price tag. If eating a fatty and protein-rich diet is better for your health, don't go broke doing it.

2. **Look for unprocessed meats.** Many meats, especially chicken and tougher cuts of beef, are labeled as "marinated." This usually means they're injected with a solution of sodium, flavor, and even sugar to tenderize the meat. Skip this. Look for meats with no additional ingredients.

3. **Cheaper cuts of meat are often better.** You don't need fancy steaks or fillets of fish to make these recipes. When making soups and stews, cooking cheaper cuts of meat (chuck, blade, pork butt/picnic) low and slow in a liquid will help tenderize the meat, so don't be afraid to look for the cheaper cuts of beef and pork.

4. **Buy bone-in and skin-on chicken.** Chicken breasts and thighs are best when purchased bone-in and with skin. Cutting the meat off the bones yourself will you save some cash, and you can freeze the bones to make broth. Chicken thighs often hold up better than breasts in soups and stews because they are fattier. If you're going to make your own bone broth or stocks, look for inexpensive beef neck bones and whole chickens. Buy these on sale for extra savings and make batches of bone broth to freeze for later.

5. **Fresh or frozen—it's all good!** Most meat is available fresh, but there's no harm in buying frozen meat and thawing it before using.

6. **Smoked meats add tons of flavor.** Smoked pork hocks, smoked sausage, smoked pork chops, and smoked pulled pork all lend extra flavor to the pot.

7. **Buy peeled and deveined shrimp.** Save yourself some time by looking for peeled and deveined shrimp. You can also find EZ-peel shrimp with the shell split down the back and the vein removed. They will slip easily out of their shells, which you can discard or save to add to a seafood broth.

## Dairy

Dairy is essential to keto. Not only does it provide plenty of flavor, but dairy products are also usually high in fat, which is important on keto. Fat helps you feel full, so you'll often hear keto dieters talk about using heavy cream or nibbling on "fat bombs," which are essentially cream cheese nuggets with additional flavors and sweetness.

If you're doing strict keto, you'll want to stick to grass-fed butter and organic dairy products. Otherwise, good-quality store brands are just fine. Always scan the ingredient labels just in case there are hidden sugars and carbs.

Dairy isn't just used for creamy soups. Some brothy soups get an added boost of flavor when topped with cheese. When you're stocking your keto refrigerator for soups and stews, the following are the ingredients to have on hand.

**Butter:** Sautéing vegetables in butter, salted or unsalted, adds a depth of flavor to soups, stews, and other recipes. Butter keeps for months in the freezer. I buy it when it's on sale and usually have about 10 pounds of it in my freezer at any given time.

**Cheese:** A multitude of different cheeses are available, and many of them will keep well in the freezer. I prefer to shred my own cheese and avoid the starchy anti-caking agents added to preshredded cheeses, but you can buy pre-shredded cheeses for convenience. I always have the following cheeses on hand.

> › **Cream cheese:** Unopened, foil-wrapped blocks of cream cheese will keep for weeks in the refrigerator. Add a dollop to thicken soups or add flavor.

> › **Extra-sharp cheddar:** Nothing has more flavor than this amazing cheese. It adds richness and a salty-nutty flavor to soups and is great for snacking.

> › **Mozzarella:** Perfect for melting into soups, adding as a garnish, or giving richness to your dish, mozzarella freezes perfectly, so you can add what you need when you need it.

> › **Parmesan:** Quality is important. Invest in a good block of Parmesan cheese, wrap it in parchment paper, and pop it into a plastic bag. It'll keep for weeks in the refrigerator, and you can shred off what you need when you need it. And those Parmesan cheese rinds? Never throw them out. Instead, add them to a soup while slowly simmering to add even more flavor.

> › **Ricotta:** Creamy and sweet, ricotta cheese is one of my favorite ingredients. It adds a luscious creaminess to soups and can be used as a garnish on top.

> › **Spicy cheese:** Havarti with chipotle or jalapeño Jack cheeses add oodles of flavor to just about any dish.

**Dairy alternatives:** If you're sensitive to dairy, you can use dairy milk alternatives such as almond milk or coconut milk. Small amounts of cashew cheese can also be used in recipes instead of cheese.

**Heavy cream:** Look for heavy cream, also known as whipping cream or 35 percent cream, that is unsweetened. With about half the carbs of regular milk, cream is often used in place of milk. Creamy soups have heavy cream in them, so keeping some on hand is essential.

**Sour cream:** Often added as a garnish or carefully added to finished soups, sour cream adds a tangy flavor and a creaminess that can't be matched. Be careful adding cold sour cream into hot soups because it could curdle. Always temper the sour cream first by adding some of the hot soup to the sour cream to warm it up and then whisking the warmed sour cream mixture back into the soup. Alternatively, add a dollop of sour cream on top of your bowl of soup and stir it in for extra richness and flavor.

# SHOULD I MAKE MY OWN BONE BROTH?

Bone broth is an essential part of keto. Not only is bone broth a healthy and wholesome meal or snack when sipped on, but it is also one of the building blocks of an amazing soup.

Though the terms are often used interchangeably, there are subtle differences between broth and stock. Bone broths are often made with meatier bones, which infuse the broth with more protein, and fewer vegetables, which allows for a purer meat flavor. Broth can be seasoned with salt and sipped. Stocks tend to be thinner because they are made with less meaty bones, and they are typically unseasoned.

I like making batches of bone broth and freezing them, and not just for sipping on cold days. Making soups with bone broth instead of stock adds another layer of flavor that turns scratch-made soups into exciting and delicious meals.

Making bone broth isn't complicated. I've included two recipes in this book: Beef Bone Broth (page 27) and Chicken Bone Broth (page 26). Each is a labor of love and is made in a slow cooker. You can adapt the recipes to a pressure cooker, but pressure cookers don't allow for natural evaporation, which helps condense the flavors in the bone broth.

My biggest tip is don't rush the recipe. To get all the collagen, protein, and flavor out of those bones, they need to steep low and slow in liquid for hours. Be patient. The results are worth it.

# THE RIGHT EQUIPMENT

You don't need any fancy equipment to make stellar soups, and you probably already have just about everything you need. I've listed most of what you'll need to outfit your kitchen with the tools to make amazing keto soups.

**Blender or immersion blender:** You'll get a smoother puree with a blender, but an immersion blender is much faster and requires less cleanup. I use both equally. If you use a blender, be careful about blending hot soups. Always leave the vent hole open (or leave the lid off entirely) and cover the top with a folded dish towel. Hot liquids tend to explode out of the blender if you're not careful.

**Cutting board:** Wood cutting boards are pretty but unsanitary. Get a good-quality, heavy, thick cutting board that is dishwasher-friendly and save yourself some cleanup time.

**Ladle:** Perfect for dishing up soups, a dishwasher-safe ladle will make serving your soups much easier.

**Measuring cup and spoons:** Having a reliable set of measuring cups and spoons is essential when cooking. Look for dishwasher-safe tools, and cleanup will be a breeze.

**Sharp knives:** Having a variety of sharp knives is essential. I like a chef's knife for chopping, a paring knife for peeling and making smaller cuts, and a slicing knife for cutting through big cuts of meat. Sharpen your knives with a sharpening steel each time before using and have them professionally sharpened every few years to maintain a good cutting edge.

**Silicone tools:** Silicone kitchen tools are some of my favorites for making soups. You don't have to worry about them melting if you leave them in a pot, and they're dishwasher safe. You can often find sets of them that include scrapers, spatulas, and whisks. They are nearly indestructible and a great investment.

**Slow cooker:** Essential for slow-cooking soups without worrying about them burning, a slow cooker is a soup maker's best friend. Get one large enough to make your favorite bone broth.

**Stock/soup pot or Dutch oven:** If using a steel pot, look for a 6- to 8-quart, heavy-bottomed pot so that you can sauté your ingredients without burning them. Dutch ovens tend to be more expensive and aren't necessary for creating amazing soups, but they will work if you already have one on hand.

# Soup Tips for Success

There's more to making soup than just tossing a bunch of ingredients into a pot, adding some broth, and letting it simmer. Building robust, flavor-packed soups with perfectly cooked ingredients (not mushy or still crunchy) takes timing. The best soups are layered with flavor, with each layer building on the next. I've got some great tips to turn you into a soup master.

**Tip 1: Always sauté the vegetables first.** Most soups follow the same formula of starting with sautéing vegetables. Using butter or avocado (or olive) oil, sauté finely chopped vegetables over medium-high heat for 5 to 6 minutes. Onions, celery, and carrots don't soften very well when cooked in liquids unless they simmer for an hour or more, so they need to be sautéed first. But be careful: You don't want to brown the vegetables, because they will discolor cream soups and lead to a bitter flavor in brothy soups. Keep an eye on the temperature and turn it down if your vegetables start to brown.

**Tip 2: Don't skip browning the proteins.** Another layer of flavor comes from caramelizing, or browning, the meat before adding it to the liquid. Sear the meat over medium-high heat until brown on all sides. It will finish cooking after it's added to the soup or stew.

**Tip 3: Season at the end of the cooking time.** Once all the ingredients in the soup pot have finished simmering, season the soup for the final time. Adjusting the salt before simmering could lead to a soup being too salty because some liquid evaporates, leaving behind a higher concentration of salt. If you season just before serving, you will get it just right.

**Tip 4: Treat dairy gently.** Dairy products, such as heavy cream and cheeses, don't like to be boiled. If you are adding cream to a soup, add it at the end of the cooking time and heat it through so that it's hot but not boiling. The same goes for cheese, which will separate and get grainy if you boil it. Even coconut milk or almond milk should be added at the end of the cooking time, unless your recipe specifically calls for adding it at a different time.

**Tip 5: Freeze leftover soup for meals in a pinch.** Many soups freeze and reheat exceptionally well. Whether freezing bone broth to add to soups or freezing the soup itself, it's is an easy way to meal prep. The best way to reheat soup is to let it thaw in the refrigerator overnight and then heat it slowly in a pot on the stovetop. Using the microwave is also an option, but watch that you don't boil soups that contain cream or cheese. I like to reuse empty sour cream and cottage cheese containers to freeze portions of soup. I label them and keep them in the freezer for several months.

# About the Recipes

Professional chefs have hours to build soups with complex flavors, and they often use a long list of ingredients. Since everyday home cooks typically don't have the luxury of that much time, I've created these recipes to have maximum flavor without taking all day to cook. Most of these recipes are easy enough to make on weeknights, while others, like the bone broths, are a labor of love that take (mostly hands-off) hours.

I've been developing recipes for years, and each one of these recipes is simple and concise, with easy-to-follow instructions. There are no mystery ingredients or complicated techniques, and you probably have nearly everything you need already in your kitchen. All of these recipes will fit with your keto lifestyle. Each has a net carb count and full macronutrient profile so that you can keep an accurate count for your daily totals. Whether you're aiming for 20 net carbs or 50, there are recipes in this book for everyone.

Soups are versatile, and if you're a year-round soup lover like me, then you'll find a wide variety of soups in this book suited to all seasons. There are cold soups for hot days and hot soups for cold days. There are soups for seafood fans, such as the brothy Manhattan Clam Chowder (page 75) and the rich and creamy Bacon and Shrimp Chowder (page 78), and picks for lovers of exotic flavors and bold spices. Some of my favorite soups are ones the whole family loves, such as the Stuffed Pepper Soup (page 53) and the Chicken and Chipotle Chowder (page 76). I've also created some soups with fun and familiar flavors, making them keto-friendly and easy to make. The Lasagna Soup (page 57) is one such recipe, and the cheesy topping for that soup is absolutely delicious.

In the final chapter, you'll find recipes for breads, crackers, and snacks that pair perfectly with any soup in this book. Like the other recipes, each of those is well-tested and easy to create.

## LABELS

To help you navigate the recipes in this book and to make sure they're fully in line with your keto lifestyle, each dairy-free, vegetarian, and vegan recipe has been appropriately labeled. You'll find these labels at the top of the recipe for easy spotting.

Some of the recipes can be made dairy-free by using coconut or almond milk instead of heavy cream, and some of the brothy soups can be made vegetarian or vegan by replacing the bone broth with vegetable stock or broth.

## TIPS

To share even more information with you, many of the recipes contain helpful tips. They include but aren't limited to easy shortcuts for prepping and cooking, advice on selecting or buying ingredients, and suggestions for adding or changing ingredients to mix things up a little. I'll also call out if ingredients can be substituted for flavor preferences, allergies, or dietary reasons.

# 2

# Bone Broths and Meaty Soups

# CHICKEN BONE BROTH

› MAKES 8 CUPS
› DAIRY-FREE

› **PREP TIME:** 15 MINUTES
› **COOK TIME:** 24 HOURS

Homemade chicken soup is a wonderful remedy for many ailments, including the common cold. Chicken bone broth contains a natural amino acid called cysteine that can improve breathing by thinning mucus in the lungs. So, whenever you have an extra chicken carcass, whip up a batch of this broth and keep it in the freezer for all of your recipes.

2 chicken carcasses, separated into pieces

1 celery stalk, chopped

1 carrot, chopped

½ yellow onion, cut into eighths

2 tablespoons apple cider vinegar

1 tablespoon avocado or olive oil

2 garlic cloves, crushed

2 bay leaves

½ teaspoon whole black peppercorns

1. In a slow cooker, combine the chicken bones, celery, carrot, onion, apple cider vinegar, oil, garlic, bay leaves, and peppercorns. Add water until the liquid reaches about 2 inches from the top of the insert.

2. Cover and cook on low for about 24 hours. Strain the broth through a fine-mesh sieve or cheesecloth folded into three layers and throw away the solids.

3. Refrigerate the broth in airtight containers for up to 5 days or freeze for up to 1 month.

## TIP

As with any stock, roasting the bones before adding them produces a better final product. (Toss the bones in oil and roast them on a sheet pan for about 30 minutes at 450°F, or until the bones are dark and fragrant but not burned.) This is not a necessary step, but you will notice the difference in the taste of the broth.

Macronutrients: Fat: 1%; Protein: 90%; Carbs: 9%
Per serving (1 cup): Calories: 45; Total fat: 0g; Total carbs: 1g; Net carbs: 1g; Fiber: 0g; Protein: 10g

# BEEF BONE BROTH

› MAKES 8 CUPS
› DAIRY-FREE

› **PREP TIME:** 15 MINUTES
› **COOK TIME:** 24 HOURS

Loaded with collagen, protein, and flavor, a good beef bone broth is one of the cornerstones of an amazing soup, but you can also drink it on its own for a hot and satisfying meal or even a delicious snack. This rich broth starts out with good, beefy bones with some meat on them, which you can get from your butcher. Don't rush it. This broth cooks low and slow for maximum flavor.

3 pounds beef bones or marrow bones

2 tablespoons avocado or olive oil

1 onion, coarsely chopped

3 celery stalks, chopped

4 garlic cloves, smashed

3 bay leaves

1 teaspoon whole black peppercorns

Water, as needed

1. Preheat the oven to 450°F.

2. Blanch the beef bones by placing them in a large pot and covering them with cold water. Then, turn the heat on high and bring the water to a boil. Reduce the heat and simmer for about 15 minutes, then remove the bones. Discard the liquid.

3. Toss the beef bones in the oil and roast them on a sheet pan for about 45 minutes or until the bones are dark and fragrant (but not burned).

4. Place the beef bones, onion, celery, garlic, bay leaves, and peppercorns into a slow cooker. Scrape any juices and crunchy bits from the sheet pan into the slow cooker. Add water until the liquid reaches about 2 inches from the top of the insert.

5. Cover and cook on low heat for about 24 hours. Strain the broth through a fine-mesh sieve or cheesecloth folded into three layers and throw away the solids.

6. Refrigerate the broth in airtight containers for up to 5 days or freeze for up to 3 months.

Macronutrients: Fat: 2%; Protein: 98%; Carbs: 0%

Per serving (1 cup): Calories: 40; Total fat: 0g; Total carbs: 0g; Net carbs: 0g; Fiber: 0g; Protein: 10g

# THAI-INSPIRED SHRIMP SOUP

› SERVES 2
› DAIRY-FREE

› **PREP TIME:** 5 MINUTES
› **COOK TIME:** 45 MINUTES

Skip the takeout and make this soup at home. It is unbelievably tasty and super simple to make. This coconut milk–based soup is aromatic and flavorful thanks to the ginger, red curry, and lime.

1 (1-inch) piece ginger, peeled

4 cups Chicken Bone Broth (page 26) or store-bought chicken broth

2 tablespoons freshly squeezed lime juice

2 tablespoons Thai red curry paste

1 cup white button mushrooms, cut into pieces

12 ounces shrimp, peeled and deveined

1 cup full-fat unsweetened coconut milk

2 tablespoons chopped fresh cilantro

1 tablespoon fish sauce

1 lime, cut into 6 wedges

1. With the back of a knife, lightly smash the ginger to release its oils and flavors.

2. In a large pot, combine the ginger, bone broth, lime juice, and red curry paste and bring to a boil over high heat. Then reduce the heat to low and simmer for 10 minutes.

3. Use a slotted spoon to remove the ginger piece from the soup. Then add the mushrooms and cook for 25 minutes.

4. Stir in the shrimp, coconut milk, cilantro, and fish sauce and cook for 2 to 3 more minutes, making sure not to overcook the shrimp.

5. Serve immediately with lime wedges.

6. Refrigerate leftovers in an airtight container for up to 3 days or freeze for up to 3 months. Store the lime wedges separately in the refrigerator.

Macronutrients: Fat: 45%; Protein: 46%; Carbs: 9%
Per serving: Calories: 518; Total fat: 26g; Total carbs: 12g; Net carbs: 8g; Fiber: 4g; Protein: 59g

# SOOTHING CHICKEN SOUP

› SERVES 4
› DAIRY-FREE

› **PREP TIME:** 15 MINUTES
› **COOK TIME:** 45 MINUTES

Basil and garlic have been shown to be antimicrobial and antibacterial, which means they can help soothe stomachaches and other digestive distress. The sodium in the broth can help replenish electrolytes that may have been lost during illness.

2 tablespoons avocado or olive oil

½ cup diced yellow onion

1 pound boneless, skinless chicken thighs, diced

1 tablespoon dried thyme

1 teaspoon pink Himalayan salt

1 teaspoon freshly ground black pepper

1½ teaspoons garlic powder

4 cups Chicken Bone Broth (page 26) or store-bought chicken broth

8 ounces fresh spinach

1 cup diced green bell peppers

1 teaspoon dried basil (optional)

1. In a large pot, heat the oil over medium heat. Add the onion and cook for about 5 minutes, stirring frequently, until translucent.

2. Add the chicken and cook for about 8 minutes, stirring occasionally. Stir in the thyme, salt, pepper, and garlic powder. Add the broth and cook for about 25 minutes.

3. Add the spinach and bell peppers and cook for another 5 minutes, or until the peppers are tender-crisp.

4. Serve the soup in bowls and sprinkle with the basil (if using).

5. Refrigerate leftovers in an airtight container for up to 5 days or freeze for up to 3 months.

### TIP

Feel free to use turkey in this recipe instead of chicken. Leftover rotisserie chicken is also a great choice, but you won't need to precook it. Simply add the cooked rotisserie chicken to the broth along with the dried thyme, garlic powder, salt, and pepper. You can also add tomatoes.

Macronutrients: Fat: 40%; Protein: 50%; Carbs: 10%

Per serving: Calories: 272; Total fat: 12g; Total carbs: 7g; Net carbs: 5g; Fiber: 2g; Protein: 34g

# TURMERIC-CHICKEN SOUP

› SERVES 4
› DAIRY-FREE

› **PREP TIME:** 5 MINUTES
› **COOK TIME:** 35 MINUTES

This soup is full of immune-boosting ingredients, including ginger, garlic, and bone broth. Turmeric is a powerhouse, and its most active compound, curcumin, is known to be an anti-inflammatory.

2 tablespoons avocado or olive oil

½ cup chopped celery, ½-inch pieces

½ cup diced yellow onion

¼ cup chopped carrots, ½-inch pieces

2 garlic cloves, minced

6 cups Chicken Bone Broth (page 26) or store-bought chicken broth

1½ tablespoons chopped fresh parsley

1 bay leaf

2 teaspoons ground turmeric

1 teaspoon curry powder

1 teaspoon grated ginger root

1 teaspoon pink Himalayan salt

8 boneless, skinless chicken thighs

2½ cups full-fat unsweetened coconut milk

2 avocados, peeled, pitted, and diced

1. In a large pot, heat the oil over medium heat. Add the celery, onion, and carrots and sauté for about 4 minutes, or until softened. Add the garlic and sauté for 1 minute.

2. Add the broth, parsley, bay leaf, turmeric, curry powder, ginger root, salt, and chicken thighs to the pot. Bring to a boil, then cover with a lid and reduce the heat to low and simmer for 10 to 15 minutes, or until the chicken is cooked through.

3. Remove the chicken and allow it to cool for 5 minutes before shredding it with two forks.

4. Whisk the coconut milk into the soup. Return the shredded chicken to the soup and stir to combine. Simmer for 5 more minutes.

5. Top each bowl with the diced avocado just before serving.

6. Refrigerate leftovers in an airtight container for 2 to 3 days or freeze for up to 3 months.

Macronutrients: Fat: 63%; Protein: 26%; Carbs: 11%

Per serving: Calories: 837; Total fat: 59g; Total carbs: 20g; Net carbs: 12g; Fiber: 8g; Protein: 54g

# PEANUT-CHICKEN SOUP

› SERVES 4
› DAIRY-FREE

› **PREP TIME:** 10 MINUTES
› **COOK TIME:** 15 MINUTES

One-pot peanut soups are popular in West Africa and South America, where they can be simple shredded greens in a rich peanut broth or a thick, complex stew with meat, spices, and coconut milk, such as this version. The finished flavor of the soup will depend on the type and amount of curry paste you use. Green curry is quite mild, but if you crave true heat in your soup, try Thai red curry paste.

2 cups Chicken Bone Broth (page 26) or store-bought chicken broth

1 cup full-fat unsweetened coconut milk

½ cup natural peanut butter

2 tablespoons curry paste, or more if desired

1 cup diced tomatoes

1 cup shredded cooked chicken breast

1 teaspoon garlic powder

1 cup shredded spinach

1 tablespoon chopped fresh cilantro

1 teaspoon pink Himalayan salt

Freshly ground black pepper

1. In a large saucepan over medium-high heat, whisk together the chicken broth, coconut milk, peanut butter, and curry paste. Bring the mixture to a boil, then reduce the heat to low and simmer for 4 minutes.

2. Stir in the tomatoes, chicken, and garlic powder and simmer for about 5 minutes, until the mixture is completely heated through.

3. Stir in the spinach and cilantro and simmer for about 2 minutes, until the greens are wilted.

4. Add the salt and season with pepper. Remove the soup from the heat and serve immediately.

5. Refrigerate leftovers in an airtight container for up to 5 days or freeze for up to 3 months.

Macronutrients: Fat: 65%; Protein: 23%; Carbs: 12%

Per serving: Calories: 426; Total fat: 30g; Total carbs: 14g; Net carbs: 10g; Fiber: 6g; Protein: 25g

# TURKEY-VEGETABLE STEW

› SERVES 6   › **PREP TIME:** 20 MINUTES
           › **COOK TIME:** 7 TO 8 HOURS

While chicken and turkey stews are very similar, turkey has a stronger, more distinctive flavor than chicken. It allows you to use more assertive seasonings, and the scent of this stew in the slow cooker will remind you of Thanksgiving or Christmas dinner.

2 tablespoons avocado or olive oil

1 pound boneless turkey breast, cut into 1-inch pieces

½ cup sliced yellow onion

2 teaspoons minced garlic

2 cups Chicken Bone Broth (page 26) or store-bought chicken broth

2 celery stalks, chopped

2 cups diced pumpkin

1 carrot, diced

1 teaspoon dried thyme

1 cup heavy (whipping) cream

Pink Himalayan salt

Freshly ground black pepper

1 scallion, white and green parts, chopped

1. In a large skillet, heat the oil over medium-high heat. Add the turkey and sauté for about 5 minutes, until browned.

2. Add the onion and garlic and sauté for an additional 3 minutes, stirring frequently.

3. Transfer the turkey mixture to the slow cooker and stir in the broth, celery, pumpkin, carrot, and thyme. Cover and cook on low for 7 to 8 hours.

4. Stir in the cream and turn the heat to high for about 10 minutes, or until the soup has heated through.

5. Season with salt and pepper and serve topped with the scallion.

6. Refrigerate leftovers in an airtight container for up to 5 days or freeze for up to 3 months.

Macronutrients: Fat: 63%; Protein: 29%; Carbs: 8%

Per serving: Calories: 301; Total fat: 21g; Total carbs: 6g; Net carbs: 5g; Fiber: 1g; Protein: 22g

# WEEKNIGHT TEXAS TURKEY CHILI

› SERVES 4

› **PREP TIME:** 15 MINUTES

› **COOK TIME:** 40 MINUTES

When the first little cold spell of the season moves in, it almost requires celebration with a pot of chili. Chili usually simmers for a few hours, but this Texas turkey chili cooks in just over a half hour and is perfect for a busy weeknight. Chili is all about the toppings, so load it up with cheese, avocado, sour cream, and scallions.

1 tablespoon avocado or olive oil

1¼ pounds lean ground turkey

½ cup diced yellow onion

½ cup diced green bell pepper

2 garlic cloves, minced

1 teaspoon pink Himalayan salt

1½ tablespoons chili powder

2 teaspoons paprika

1 teaspoon garlic powder

½ teaspoon dried Mexican oregano

½ teaspoon ground cumin

1 (14-ounce) can diced tomatoes

1½ cups Chicken Bone Broth (page 26) or store-bought chicken broth

1 tablespoon tomato paste

Shredded cheese, for garnish (optional)

Sour cream, for garnish (optional)

Diced avocado, for garnish (optional)

Sliced scallions, both green and white parts, for garnish (optional)

1. In a large pot or Dutch oven, heat the oil over medium-high heat. Add the turkey, onion, bell pepper, garlic, and salt. Crumbling the turkey with a spatula, cook for about 8 minutes, or until the turkey is brown and cooked through.

2. Stir in the chili powder, paprika, garlic powder, oregano, and cumin and cook for 1 minute.

3. Stir in the tomatoes and their juices, broth, and tomato paste. Simmer, uncovered, for 30 minutes or until the flavors have combined, the vegetables are tender, and the sauce has thickened a bit.

4. Serve topped with shredded cheese, sour cream, avocado, and scallions (if using).

5. Refrigerate leftovers and garnishes separately in airtight containers for up to 5 days or freeze for up to 3 months.

Macronutrients: Fat: 62%; Protein: 28%; Carbs: 10%

Per serving (includes garnishes): Calories: 514; Total fat: 36g; Total carbs: 14g; Net carbs: 6g; Fiber: 8g; Protein: 37g

# TUSCAN MEATBALL SOUP

> SERVES 4

> **PREP TIME:** 15 MINUTES
> **COOK TIME:** 30 MINUTES

This soup gets an Italian flair from the homemade meatballs that cook beautifully in the broth. The vegetables in this soup, such as the onion, carrots, and kale, pump up the vitamin and mineral content. The result is pure soup perfection.

**For the meatballs**

1 pound lean ground beef

1 large egg, beaten

2 garlic cloves, minced

1 tablespoon chopped fresh parsley

1 tablespoon chopped fresh basil

½ teaspoon pink Himalayan salt

¼ teaspoon freshly ground black pepper

2 tablespoons avocado or olive oil

**For the soup**

2 tablespoons avocado or olive oil

1 yellow onion, diced

1 large carrot, cut into ½-inch pieces

2 garlic cloves, minced

6 cups Beef Bone Broth (page 27) or store-bought beef broth

2 bay leaves

1 cup stemmed and chopped kale

1 cup heavy (whipping) cream

Pink Himalayan salt

Freshly ground black pepper

2 avocados, peeled, pitted, and diced

1 tablespoon chopped fresh parsley

**To make the meatballs**

1. In a large bowl, combine the ground beef, egg, garlic, parsley, basil, salt, and pepper. Use your hands to gently mix until well incorporated.

2. Using your hands, roll the meat mixture into about 20 small balls about 1½ inches in diameter.

3. In a large sauté pan or skillet, heat the oil over medium heat. Cook the meatballs for 3 to 4 minutes, turning frequently, until all sides are brown. Set aside.

**To make the soup**

4. In a large pot, heat the oil over medium heat. Add the onion, carrot, and garlic and cook until onions are translucent, about 5 minutes. Stir frequently.

5. Add the broth, meatballs, and bay leaves to the pot. Bring to a boil, reduce the heat to low, and simmer for 5 minutes.

6. Add the kale and simmer until the meatballs are cooked through, about 5 to 7 minutes.

7. Stir in the cream, turn the heat back up to high, and heat the soup through without boiling it. Turn off the heat.

8. Season with salt and pepper before serving. Top with the diced avocados and parsley.

9. Refrigerate leftovers and garnishes separately in airtight containers for up to 5 days or freeze for up to 3 months.

## TIP

This soup also tastes great with a spoonful of pesto stirred in.

Macronutrients: Fat: 71%; Protein: 21%; Carbs: 8%

Per serving: Calories: 803; Total fat: 63g; Total carbs: 16g; Net carbs: 8g; Fiber: 8g; Protein: 43g

# ITALIAN SAUSAGE SOUP

› MAKES 4 SERVINGS    › **PREP TIME:** 5 MINUTES
                      › **COOK TIME:** 30 MINUTES

Soup is wonderful, especially in the fall and winter. This recipe makes a slightly spicy, comforting, and delicious Italian sausage soup that is the perfect cold-weather meal with a nice big salad on the side.

1 tablespoon avocado or olive oil

½ yellow onion, diced

3 garlic cloves, minced

8 ounces hot Italian sausage, removed from their casings

2 cups Chicken Bone Broth (page 26) or store-bought chicken broth

1 (14.5-ounce) can diced tomatoes

1 teaspoon red pepper flakes

1 teaspoon dried oregano

1 teaspoon dried basil

Pink Himalayan salt

Freshly ground black pepper

¼ cup freshly grated Parmesan cheese, divided

2 cups chopped fresh spinach

1.  In a large saucepan, heat the oil over medium heat. Sauté the onion and garlic for 5 to 7 minutes until the onion is soft and translucent.

2.  Add the sausage to the pan. Cook for about 5 minutes as you crumble it, allowing the meat to brown.

3.  Stir in the chicken broth and tomatoes and their juices. Bring to a boil, then reduce the heat to low.

4.  Add the red pepper flakes, oregano, and basil. Season with salt and pepper and stir in 2 tablespoons of Parmesan. Simmer for 10 minutes, then remove from the heat.

5.  Stir in the spinach until wilted. Sprinkle each serving with the remaining 2 tablespoons of Parmesan.

6.  Refrigerate leftovers in an airtight container for up to 5 days or freeze for up to 3 months.

Macronutrients: Fat: 67%; Protein: 21%; Carbs: 12%

Per serving: Calories: 311; Total fat: 23g; Total carbs: 10g; Net carbs: 9g; Fiber: 3g; Protein: 16g

# CREAMY CAULIFLOWER-SAUSAGE SOUP

› SERVES 4

› **PREP TIME:** 5 MINUTES
› **COOK TIME:** 50 MINUTES

This creamy cauliflower and sausage soup is the perfect option if you are looking for a hearty and filling meal. Make sure to use pork sausage with no added sugars and artificial ingredients, or use ground pork. Both taste great and pair amazingly well with the cauliflower and garlic.

1 tablespoon avocado or olive oil

1½ pounds no-sugar-added pork sausage or ground pork

½ cup diced yellow onion

4 garlic cloves, minced

6 cups Chicken Bone Broth (page 26) or store-bought chicken broth

1 cauliflower head, chopped into florets (about 4 cups)

3 thyme sprigs, plus more for garnish

1 bay leaf

1 teaspoon pink Himalayan salt

1 cup heavy (whipping) cream

1. In a large pot, heat the oil over medium-high heat. Add the pork sausage and, crumbling the meat, sauté it until it is cooked through and browned, about 8 minutes.

2. Remove the sausage from the pot with a slotted spoon and set it aside, leaving behind the sausage grease.

3. In the same pot, add the onion and garlic and sauté, stirring constantly, until the onion is softened, about 5 minutes.

4. Add the bone broth, cauliflower, thyme, bay leaf, and salt to the pot. Cover and cook for 30 minutes or until the cauliflower is completely tender.

5. Remove the bay leaf and thyme sprigs. Using an immersion blender, blend the soup until completely smooth. If you don't have an immersion blender, carefully transfer the soup to a blender in batches, puree it, and add it back into the pot.

6. Whisk in the cream and stir the sausage back into the soup. Cook over low heat until heated through. Serve.

7. Refrigerate leftovers in an airtight container for up to 5 days or freeze for up to 3 months.

Macronutrients: Fat: 70%; Protein: 24%; Carbs: 6%

Per serving: Calories: 794; Total fat: 62g; Total carbs: 12g; Net carbs: 9g; Fiber: 3g; Protein: 47g

# CHEESEBURGER SOUP

› SERVES 8

› **PREP TIME:** 15 MINUTES
› **COOK TIME:** 6 HOURS

Cheeseburger soup is a classic family favorite in many homes, and it can be made perfectly in a slow cooker with very little prep time. If you have never had this dish, the taste of your favorite burger in a bowl is a wonderful surprise. Top it with a little diced tomato and chopped pickles for a real burger experience.

2 tablespoons avocado or olive oil

1 pound lean ground beef

½ cup diced yellow onion

2 teaspoons minced garlic

6 cups Beef Bone Broth (page 27) or store-bought beef broth

1 (28-ounce) can diced tomatoes

1 cup diced celery

½ cup diced carrot

2 cups shredded cheddar cheese

1 cup heavy (whipping) cream

½ teaspoon freshly ground black pepper

1 scallion, both white and green parts, chopped

1.  In a large skillet, heat the oil over medium-high heat. Add the ground beef and sauté until it is cooked through, about 6 minutes.

2.  Add the onion and garlic and sauté for an additional 3 minutes.

3.  Transfer the beef mixture to the slow cooker and stir in the broth, tomatoes and their juices, celery, and carrot. Cover and cook on low for 6 hours.

4.  Stir in the cheese, cream, and pepper. Serve hot, topped with the scallion.

5.  Refrigerate leftovers in an airtight container for up to 5 days or freeze for up to 3 months.

## TIP

Hamburger soup can be just as delicious as cheeseburger soup, although you will lose some of the fat grams. For a dairy-free version, instead of the cheese, add a cup of crispy cooked bacon and change the cream to coconut milk.

Macronutrients: Fat: 65%; Protein: 27%; Carbs: 8%

Per serving: Calories: 414; Total fat: 30g; Total carbs: 8g; Net carbs: 5g; Fiber: 3g; Protein: 28g

# PIZZA SOUP

› SERVES 4

› **PREP TIME:** 10 MINUTES
› **COOK TIME:** 20 MINUTES

If you're a pizza fan, then you're going to love this soup. With all the flavors of your favorite pizza but none of the carbs, this hearty, satisfying, and wholesome soup is one the entire family will love. You can also add your favorite pizza ingredients, such as mushrooms, peppers, olives, and cooked sausage. This soup is perfect for lunch or dinner, and it freezes like a dream.

1 tablespoon avocado or olive oil

½ cup diced yellow onion

4 cups Beef Bone Broth (page 27) or store-bought beef broth

1 (14.5-ounce) can diced tomatoes

4 ounces pepperoni slices, quartered

½ cup diced green bell pepper

1 tablespoon Italian seasoning

1 teaspoon pink Himalayan salt

¼ teaspoon freshly ground black pepper

½ cup shredded mozzarella cheese

1.  In a large soup pot, heat the oil over medium-high heat. Sauté the onion for 4 to 5 minutes, until it is soft and translucent.

2.  Add the broth and tomatoes and their juices to the pot and bring to a boil.

3.  Reduce the heat to low and add the pepperoni, bell pepper, Italian seasoning, salt, and pepper. Simmer for 10 minutes.

4.  Serve the soup, garnishing each bowl with 2 tablespoons of shredded mozzarella before serving.

5.  Refrigerate leftovers in an airtight container for up to 1 week or freeze for up to 3 months.

## TIP

Save yourself some preparation time by using mini pepperoni, which are often found in the deli section of grocery stores.

Macronutrients: Fat: 60%; Protein: 30%; Carbs: 10%

Per serving: Calories: 283; Total fat: 19g; Total carbs: 7g; Net carbs: 4g; Fiber: 3g; Protein: 21g

# BEEF AND VEGETABLE SOUP

› SERVES 4
› DAIRY-FREE

› **PREP TIME:** 10 MINUTES
› **COOK TIME:** 45 MINUTES

This soup is an instant classic. This is an old-fashioned beef stew without the thickening agents (such as flour). It also provides healing power thanks to the scratch-made Beef Bone Broth (page 27). The stew beef gets more tender the longer it cooks, so the more time you let this soup simmer, the better.

4 tablespoons avocado or olive oil, divided

1½ pounds stew beef, cut into ½-inch chunks

Pink Himalayan salt

Freshly ground black pepper

½ cup chopped celery, ½-inch pieces

½ cup diced yellow onion

¼ cup chopped carrots, ½-inch pieces

2 garlic cloves, minced

6 cups Beef Bone Broth (page 27) or store-bought beef broth

1 (14-ounce) can diced tomatoes

1 tablespoon chopped fresh parsley

1 teaspoon dried oregano

½ teaspoon dried thyme

1. In a large pot, heat 2 tablespoons of oil over medium heat. Use paper towels to dab the stew beef dry, then season with salt and pepper. In batches, add the beef to the pot and brown on each side, about 4 minutes. Transfer the browned beef to a plate and set aside.

2. In the same large pot, heat the remaining 2 tablespoons of oil over medium heat. Add the celery, onion, and carrots and sauté for about 4 minutes, or until softened. Add the garlic and sauté for 1 minute.

3. Add the broth, tomatoes and their juices, parsley, oregano, thyme, and beef to the pot. Bring to a boil, then cover with a lid and reduce the heat to low. Simmer for 30 minutes, then serve.

4. Refrigerate leftovers in an airtight container for up to 5 days or freeze for up to 3 months.

Macronutrients: Fat: 50%; Protein: 43%; Carbs: 7%

Per serving: Calories: 397; Total fat: 21g; Total carbs: 8g; Net carbs: 3g; Fiber: 5g; Protein: 44g

# BEEF AND PUMPKIN STEW

› SERVES 6
› DAIRY-FREE

› **PREP TIME:** 15 MINUTES
› **COOK TIME:** 8 HOURS
ON LOW

Tender chunks of beef in rich gravy are perfect when served over fluffy mashed cauliflower at the end of a long day. The scent of this stew cooking when you open your door will draw you to the kitchen before you have taken off your coat. This recipe tastes even better the next day and freezes beautifully, so it is very convenient for meal planning.

1 (2-pound) beef chuck roast, cut into 1-inch chunks

½ teaspoon pink Himalayan salt

¼ teaspoon freshly ground black pepper

2 tablespoons avocado or olive oil

2 cups Beef Bone Broth (page 27) or store-bought beef broth

1½ cups cubed pumpkin, cut into 1-inch chunks

1 cup diced tomatoes

½ cup diced yellow onion

¼ cup apple cider vinegar

2 teaspoons minced garlic

1 teaspoon dried thyme

1 tablespoon chopped fresh parsley

1. Lightly season the beef chunks with the salt and pepper. In a large skillet, heat the oil over medium-high heat. Add the beef and brown on all sides, about 7 minutes.

2. Transfer the beef to the slow cooker and stir in the broth, pumpkin, tomatoes, onion, apple cider vinegar, garlic, and thyme. Cover and cook on low for about 8 hours, until the beef is very tender.

3. Serve topped with the parsley.

4. Refrigerate leftovers in an airtight container for up to 5 days.

## TIP

This recipe would be enhanced by replacing ½ cup of the beef broth with ½ cup of dry red wine. Red wine adds depth to the flavor and, in this amount, adds less than ½ gram of carbs per serving.

Macronutrients: Fat: 60%; Protein: 37%; Carbs: 3%

Per serving: Calories: 340; Total fat: 22g; Total carbs: 5g; Net carbs: 4g; Fiber: 1g; Protein: 32g

**SLOW-COOKER
CHICKEN POZOLE**

Page 45

# 3

# Faux Pasta, Rice, and Grain Soups

# CHICKEN ZOODLE SOUP

> SERVES 4
> DAIRY-FREE

> **PREP TIME:** 20 MINUTES
> **COOK TIME:** 15 MINUTES

This soul-satisfying soup is loaded with nutrients from fresh vegetables and bone broth, and it's simple to throw together. It can also be a great way to use up any leftover veggies you have on hand. Just sauté them with the garlic, onion, and celery for an even more filling dish. You can make your own zucchini noodles ("zoodles") by using a handheld spiralizer or vegetable peeler, or purchase precut zucchini noodles, fresh or frozen, at your local grocery store.

2 tablespoons avocado or olive oil

2 baby carrots, diced

2 celery stalks, diced

¼ cup diced yellow onion

1 garlic clove, minced

4 cups Chicken Bone Broth (page 26) or store-bought chicken broth

2 cups shredded rotisserie chicken

½ teaspoon dried thyme

½ teaspoon dried oregano

2 cups zucchini noodles

Pink Himalayan salt

Freshly ground black pepper

1. In a large saucepan, heat the oil over medium heat. Add the carrots and cook for 2 minutes.

2. Stir in the celery, onion, and garlic and cook until softened, about 5 minutes.

3. Stir in the broth, chicken, thyme, and oregano until well combined. Add the zoodles and stir again.

4. Bring the soup to a boil, then reduce the heat to low and simmer for about 1 minute or until the zoodles are cooked but still have a little crunch. Season with salt and pepper.

5. Divide the soup into bowls and serve immediately.

6. Refrigerate leftovers in an airtight container for up to 4 days or freeze for up to 3 months.

Macronutrients: Fat: 41%; Protein: 49%; Carbs: 10%

Per serving: Calories: 251; Total fat: 11g; Total carbs: 7g; Net carbs: 5g; Fiber: 2g; Protein: 31g

# SLOW-COOKER CHICKEN POZOLE

› SERVES 4
› DAIRY-FREE

› **PREP TIME:** 5 MINUTES
› **COOK TIME:** 6 TO 8 HOURS

Think of this as an upgraded classic chicken soup with fresh veggies, healing bone broth, and Mexican spices. It's so easy to make. Just throw the ingredients in the slow cooker and let them simmer all day.

2 tablespoons avocado or olive oil

½ cup diced yellow onion

2 poblano peppers, seeded and chopped

2 garlic cloves, minced

6 cups Chicken Bone Broth (page 26) or store-bought chicken broth

4 boneless, skinless chicken thighs

1 tablespoon ground cumin

1 tablespoon dried oregano

2 teaspoons chili powder

2 teaspoons pink Himalayan salt

½ teaspoon freshly ground black pepper

2 cups cauliflower rice

2 avocados, peeled, pitted, and diced

2 red radishes, sliced

2 tablespoons chopped fresh cilantro

1. In a large sauté pan or skillet, heat the oil over medium heat. Add the onion and peppers and sauté for about 4 minutes, or until softened.

2. Add the garlic and sauté for another minute. Transfer the sautéed veggies to a slow cooker and place the bone broth, chicken thighs, cumin, oregano, chili powder, salt, and pepper into the slow cooker. Cook on low for 6 to 8 hours.

3. Remove the chicken and allow it to cool for 5 minutes before shredding it with two forks. Return the shredded chicken to the slow cooker along with the cauliflower rice and cook for another 10 minutes.

4. Transfer the soup to a large bowl and garnish with the avocado, radish, and cilantro before serving.

5. Refrigerate leftovers in an airtight container for up to 5 days or freeze for up to 3 months.

Macronutrients: Fat: 51%; Protein: 34%; Carbs: 15%

Per serving: Calories: 479; Total fat: 27g; Total carbs: 18g; Net carbs: 9g; Fiber: 9g; Protein: 41g

# CHICKEN SHIRATAKI RAMEN

› SERVES 4
› DAIRY-FREE

› **PREP TIME:** 25 MINUTES
› **COOK TIME:** 30 MINUTES

Traditional Japanese ramen includes broth, meat, vegetables, and non-keto-friendly noodles. This recipe packs the same savory punch as the thrifty soup you may have had during college or growing up, but it replaces the starchy dried noodles with shirataki noodles. If you cannot find coconut aminos, use low-sodium soy sauce.

2 packages shirataki noodles

4 ounces shiitake mushrooms

1 tablespoon avocado or olive oil, plus 1 teaspoon, divided

½ teaspoon pink Himalayan salt

4 chicken bouillon cubes

4 cups water

3½ tablespoons shredded carrots

2 garlic cloves, minced

¼ teaspoon ground ginger

2½ tablespoons coconut aminos or soy sauce

2 cups shredded rotisserie chicken

4 soft-boiled large eggs, halved

1 scallion, white part only, diced (optional)

Hot sauce (optional)

1.  Preheat the oven to 400°F. Line a baking sheet with paper towels. Line a separate baking sheet with parchment paper.

2.  Rinse and drain the noodles thoroughly. Place them on the baking sheet lined with paper towels and cover with more paper towels. Gently press to soak up the water. Discard the top layer of paper towels and let the noodles air-dry for 20 minutes.

3.  Meanwhile, place the mushrooms (stems and caps) on the baking sheet lined with parchment paper and drizzle evenly with 1 teaspoon of oil. Sprinkle with the salt. Bake for 20 minutes, until tender. Set aside.

4.  While the mushrooms are cooking, in a medium saucepan, heat the bouillon cubes and water over medium-high heat until the bouillon dissolves. Turn off the heat.

5.  In a large saucepan, heat the remaining 1 tablespoon of oil over medium heat. Add the carrots, garlic, and ginger, stirring frequently so the garlic does not burn. Cook until fragrant, 1 to 2 minutes.

6.  Add the noodles and stir-fry for another 2 to 3 minutes. Add the prepared bouillon, coconut aminos, and chicken. Bring the mixture to a boil, then reduce the heat to low and simmer for 5 minutes.

7. Divide the soup equally into four bowls. Top each bowl of ramen with a halved egg, equal portions of mushrooms, and equal portions of scallions (if using). Drizzle with hot sauce (if using) before serving.

8. Refrigerate leftovers in an airtight container for up to 4 days.

**TIP**

Swap the chicken bouillon for beef bouillon and trade the chicken for a 1-pound cooked, sliced flank steak. Or go vegetarian by using vegetable bouillon and using 2 cups of bok choy instead of chicken.

Macronutrients: Fat: 45%; Protein: 38%; Carbs: 17%

Per serving (1 cup): Calories: 286; Total fat: 15g; Total carbs: 13g; Net carbs: 6g; Fiber: 7g; Protein: 29g

# HOMESTYLE CHICKEN AND DUMPLING SOUP

> SERVES 6

> **PREP TIME:** 20 MINUTES
> **COOK TIME:** 45 MINUTES

Dumplings are traditionally poached in the broth, which helps thicken the soup. However, for this keto version, the dumplings are baked so that they hold up in the soup and there is better portion control. Chicken and dumplings should be creamy, so the soup is thickened with pureed cauliflower.

**For the dumplings**

¾ cup almond flour

¼ cup coconut flour

½ teaspoon baking powder

¼ teaspoon kosher salt

⅛ teaspoon freshly ground black pepper

⅛ teaspoon poultry seasoning

3 large eggs, lightly beaten

⅓ cup shredded mozzarella cheese

2½ tablespoons unsalted butter, melted

**For the chicken stew**

1½ tablespoons unsalted butter

1½ cup diced celery

½ cup diced yellow onion

1 teaspoon pink Himalayan salt

2 garlic cloves, finely minced

½ teaspoon poultry seasoning

1½ teaspoons dried parsley

¼ teaspoon dried thyme

5 cups Chicken Bone Broth (page 26) or store-bought chicken broth

2 cups cauliflower florets

¼ cup water

¾ cup heavy (whipping) cream

3 ounces cream cheese

3 cups cooked chicken or turkey

**To make the dumplings**

1. Preheat the oven to 350°F. Line a baking sheet with parchment paper. Set aside.

2. In a large bowl, stir together the almond and coconut flours, baking powder, salt, pepper, and poultry seasoning. Stir in the eggs, cheese, and melted butter until fully incorporated. Let rest for 5 minutes.

3. Using a cookie scoop or spoon, scoop the dough onto the prepared baking sheet, making about 18 dumplings. Roll each portion into a ball, if desired.

4. Bake for 10 to 12 minutes, or until slightly golden on top. Set aside.

**To make the chicken stew**

5. In a large pot or Dutch oven, melt the butter over medium heat. Add the celery, onion, and salt. Cook for 5 to 7 minutes until the vegetables are tender. Add the garlic, poultry seasoning, parsley, and thyme. Cook for 1 minute more. Add the broth and simmer, uncovered, for 20 minutes.

6. In a medium microwave-safe bowl, combine the cauliflower and water. Cover tightly with plastic wrap and microwave on high power for 5 to 7 minutes, or until tender. Transfer the cauliflower to a blender and add the heavy cream and cream cheese. Blend on high speed until smooth and creamy. Add the cauliflower mixture to the stock and vegetable mixture. Stir to combine.

7. Add the chicken and cook for about 5 minutes, or until heated through.

8. Place 3 dumplings in a bowl and ladle about 1 cup of chicken stew over the dumplings.

9. Refrigerate leftover soup and dumplings separately in airtight containers for up to 5 days or freeze for up to 3 months.

### TIP

Only have frozen cauliflower on hand? No problem. Simply cook the florets for 1 to 2 minutes more, or until tender.

Macronutrients: Fat: 70%; Protein: 24%; Carbs: 6%
Per serving: Calories: 577; Total fat: 45g; Total carbs: 9g; Net carbs: 3g; Fiber: 6g; Protein: 34g

# GREEK CHICKEN, "RICE," AND ARTICHOKE SOUP

› SERVES 4
› DAIRY-FREE

› **PREP TIME:** 10 MINUTES
› **COOK TIME:** 15 MINUTES

Avgolemono is a classic sauce similar to hollandaise, made from egg yolks and lemon juice, that is common in Greek, Turkish, Jewish, and Italian cuisines. Here, oil is added for richness, and the sauce serves as a flavorful base for a chicken soup that is simple enough to be made midweek. Riced cauliflower adds bulk and a great texture. For ease, use store-bought rotisserie chicken, but feel free to use any leftover cooked chicken you may have on hand.

4 cups Chicken Bone Broth (page 26) or store-bought chicken broth

2 cups riced cauliflower, divided

2 large egg yolks

¼ cup freshly squeezed lemon juice (about 2 lemons)

¾ cup avocado or olive oil, divided

8 ounces cooked chicken, coarsely chopped

1 (13.75-ounce) can artichoke hearts, drained and quartered

1 teaspoon pink Himalayan salt

¼ cup chopped fresh dill

1. In a large saucepan over medium-high heat, bring the broth to a low boil. Reduce the heat to low, cover, and simmer for 2 minutes.

2. Transfer 1 cup of the hot broth to a blender or food processor. Add ½ cup of raw riced cauliflower, the egg yolks, and the lemon juice and puree. While the processor or blender is running, stream in ½ cup of oil and blend until smooth.

3. Whisking constantly, pour the puree into the simmering stock until well blended and smooth. Add the chicken and artichokes and simmer until thickened slightly, 8 to 10 minutes.

4. Stir in the salt, the dill, and the remaining 1½ cups of riced cauliflower. Serve warm, drizzled with the remaining ¼ cup of oil.

5. Refrigerate leftovers in an airtight container for 2 to 3 days.

Macronutrients: Fat: 70%; Protein: 21%; Carbs: 9%

Per serving: Calories: 563; Total fat: 43g; Total carbs: 14g; Net carbs: 10g; Fiber: 4g; Protein: 30g

# JAMBALAYA SOUP

› SERVES 8

› **PREP TIME:** 15 MINUTES

› **COOK TIME:** 6 TO
7 HOURS ON LOW

Jambalaya is a traditional Cajun and Creole spicy rice dish from Louisiana and is influenced by both Spanish and French cuisine. This recipe is based on the Cajun version and is bursting with chicken, sausage, and shrimp. The flavors and textures work well as a soup, and it is just as filling as its rice-based counterpart. Keep in mind that the more jalapeño seeds you add to this soup, the spicier it will become, so adjust according to your preference. If you do not have time at the end of the cooking process to wait 30 minutes for raw shrimp to cook, you can use small precooked shrimp instead. Let them heat up in the steaming broth while you set your table.

6 cups Chicken Bone Broth (page 26) or store-bought chicken broth

1 (28-ounce) can diced tomatoes

1 pound spicy andouille sausage, sliced

1 cup chopped cooked chicken

1 red bell pepper, chopped

½ yellow onion, chopped

3 tablespoons Cajun seasoning

1 jalapeño pepper, seeded and chopped

1 tablespoon avocado or olive oil

2 teaspoons minced garlic

8 ounces medium shrimp, peeled, deveined, and chopped

½ cup sour cream

1 avocado, peeled, pitted, and diced

2 tablespoons chopped cilantro

1. In a slow cooker, combine the broth, tomatoes and their juices, sausage, chicken, bell pepper, onion, Cajun seasoning, jalapeño pepper, oil, and garlic. Cover and cook on low for 6 to 7 hours.

2. Stir in the shrimp and leave on low for 30 minutes, or until the shrimp are cooked through.

3. Serve topped with the sour cream, avocado, and cilantro.

4. Refrigerate leftovers and garnishes separately in airtight containers for 2 to 3 days or freeze for up to 3 months.

Macronutrients: Fat: 60%; Protein: 29%; Carbs: 11%

Per serving: Calories: 394; Total fat: 26g; Total carbs: 11g; Net carbs: 7g; Fiber: 4g; Protein: 29g

# CHICKEN AND CAULI RICE SOUP

› SERVES 6 TO 8
› DAIRY-FREE

› **PREP TIME:** 30 MINUTES
› **COOK TIME:** 30 MINUTES

There's nothing like the comforting aroma of a big pot of chicken soup simmering on the stove, and it seems every Southerner has their own version. This version is spiced with warm, Mexican-inspired flavors and is completely dairy-free.

2 tablespoons avocado or olive oil

¾ cup diced celery with leaves

½ cup diced yellow onion

1½ teaspoons pink Himalayan salt, divided

1 cup diced zucchini

3 garlic cloves, minced

2 tablespoons chili powder

1 tablespoon dried parsley

1¼ teaspoons granulated garlic

1¼ teaspoons ground cumin

1¼ teaspoons paprika

½ teaspoon freshly ground black pepper

½ teaspoon dried Mexican oregano

6 cups Chicken Bone Broth (page 26) or store-bought chicken broth

3 cups shredded cooked chicken thighs

2 (12-ounce) packages frozen cauliflower rice

Chopped fresh cilantro, for garnish

Diced avocado, for garnish (optional)

1. In a large stockpot, heat the oil over medium heat. Add the celery, onion, and ½ teaspoon of salt. Sauté for about 5 minutes, or until tender.

2. Add the zucchini, garlic, chili powder, parsley, granulated garlic, cumin, paprika, the remaining 1 teaspoon of salt, the pepper, and the oregano. Cook for 1 to 2 minutes more, stirring constantly.

3. Stir in the broth. Bring the mixture to a boil, then reduce the heat to low. Simmer, uncovered, for 10 to 15 minutes.

4. Add the chicken and cauliflower rice. Simmer for 10 minutes more, or until the vegetables are tender. Serve warm, topped with cilantro and avocado (if using).

5. Refrigerate leftovers in an airtight container for up to 4 days or freeze for up to 3 months.

Macronutrients: Fat: 48%; Protein: 39%; Carbs: 13%

Per serving: Calories: 287; Total fat: 15g; Total carbs: 10g; Net carbs: 6g; Fiber: 4g; Protein: 28g

# STUFFED PEPPER SOUP

› SERVES 4

› **PREP TIME:** 10 MINUTES
› **COOK TIME:** 35 MINUTES

Stuffed bell peppers are a much-loved but time-consuming dish. Now you can get all the flavors of this timeless classic in soup form. Hearty, warm, and comforting, this soup is loaded with protein and fiber-rich vegetables, making it a great pick for lunch or supper. The flavors are even better when the leftover soup is heated up the next day.

1 tablespoon avocado or olive oil

½ cup diced yellow onion

1 pound lean ground beef

½ teaspoon garlic powder

½ teaspoon dried oregano

1 (28-ounce) can crushed tomatoes

2 cups Beef Bone Broth (page 27) or store-bought beef broth

1½ cups cauliflower rice

1 cup diced green bell pepper

½ teaspoon pink Himalayan salt

¼ teaspoon freshly ground black pepper

½ cup shredded mozzarella cheese, divided

1. In a large skillet, heat the oil over medium-high heat and add the onion. Cook for 4 to 5 minutes, stirring frequently, or until the onion is soft and translucent.

2. Add the ground beef and cook for about 8 minutes until no longer pink, breaking it up as you cook it. Remove from the heat and discard any fat in the pan. Add the garlic powder and oregano and mix well to combine.

3. Add the onion and ground beef mixture to a large soup pot. Add the tomatoes and their juices and the broth. Bring to a simmer over low heat and cook, covered, for 15 minutes.

4. Add the cauliflower rice and bell pepper and simmer for an additional 5 minutes. Season with the salt and pepper.

5. Divide the soup into bowls and top each serving with about 2 tablespoons of mozzarella cheese before serving.

6. Refrigerate leftovers in an airtight container for up to 4 days or freeze for up to 3 months.

Macronutrients: Fat: 48%; Protein: 38%; Carbs: 14%

Per serving: Calories: 359; Total fat: 19g; Total carbs: 13g; Net carbs: 7g; Fiber: 6g; Protein: 34g

# ITALIAN WEDDING SOUP

> SERVES 4

> **PREP TIME:** 15 MINUTES
> **COOK TIME:** 30 MINUTES

Italian wedding soup is an Italian American staple that's found in many restaurants, and you can even buy it canned from your grocery store. However, the traditional version is loaded with carbs from pasta and high-carb veggies. This version is packed with all the same flavors, but you can enjoy it guilt-free on your keto diet.

**For the meatballs**

1 pound lean ground pork

1 large egg

1 tablespoon Italian seasoning

½ teaspoon pink Himalayan salt

1 tablespoon avocado or olive oil

**For the soup**

1 tablespoon avocado or olive oil

½ cup diced yellow onion

½ cup diced celery

1 garlic clove, minced

6 cups Chicken Bone Broth (page 26) or store-bought chicken broth

1 teaspoon dried oregano

1 teaspoon dried basil

5 ounces fresh baby spinach

½ teaspoon pink Himalayan salt

½ cup grated Parmesan cheese

**To make the meatballs**

1. In a medium bowl, use your hands or a large wooden spoon to mix the ground pork with the egg, Italian seasoning, and salt. The mixture will be fairly wet, but don't worry. Form the mixture into about 50 meatballs, about ½ inch in diameter.

2. In a large skillet, heat the oil over medium heat. Working in batches, brown the meatballs for 1 to 2 minutes per side, then flip them over and repeat. You won't get all the sides browned, and they may end up more oval in shape, but that's okay. Cook the meatballs until they're golden brown, about 10 minutes in total. Remove them from the pan and set aside.

**To make the soup**

3. In the same skillet, heat the oil over medium heat. Add the onion and celery and cook for 4 to 5 minutes, stirring frequently, until the onion and celery are soft and translucent. Add the garlic and cook for 1 minute more.

4. Scrape the garlic, onion, and celery into a large soup pot. Add the broth and bring to a boil over high heat, then reduce the heat to low and simmer.

5. Add the oregano and basil and gently lower the meatballs into the broth. Simmer for 10 minutes, uncovered.

6.  Turn off the heat, add the baby spinach and salt, and stir well to incorporate. Divide the soup into bowls and top each with 2 tablespoons of Parmesan before serving.

7.  Refrigerate leftovers in an airtight container for up to 1 week or freeze for up to 3 months.

Macronutrients: Fat: 63%; Protein: 32%; Carbs: 5%

Per serving: Calories: 516; Total fat: 36g; Total carbs: 7g; Net carbs: 5g; Fiber: 2g; Protein: 41g

# CREAMY CHICKEN AND RICE SOUP

› SERVES 4

› **PREP TIME:** 10 MINUTES
› **COOK TIME:** 25 MINUTES

Rice is a no-no on keto, but by replacing starchy rice with shirataki rice, you can get all the flavor and texture of this classic soup without the carbs. Thicken the soup with xanthan gum for a creamier, more luxurious soup. Total comfort food, this hearty soup is perfect on a cold day or whenever you need a hug in a bowl.

1 tablespoon avocado or olive oil

½ cup diced yellow onion

½ cup diced celery

½ cup diced carrot

1 garlic clove, minced

4 cups Chicken Bone Broth (page 26) or store-bought chicken broth

½ teaspoon dried thyme

1½ cups diced cooked chicken

1 cup shirataki rice, drained and well rinsed

1 cup heavy (whipping) cream

½ teaspoon pink Himalayan salt

¼ teaspoon ground white pepper

½ teaspoon xanthan gum (optional)

1.  In a large pot, heat the oil over medium-high heat and add the onion, celery, and carrot. Cook for 4 to 5 minutes, stirring frequently, or until the vegetables are soft and translucent. Add the garlic and cook for 1 minute more.

2.  Add the broth and thyme to the pot, then turn the heat up to high and allow the soup to boil. Then, reduce the heat to low and simmer, covered, for 15 minutes.

3.  Remove the lid and add the chicken and shirataki rice. Bring to a simmer and cook for 5 minutes. Turn off the heat and add the cream, mixing well to incorporate. Season with the salt and pepper. To thicken, whisk in the xanthan gum (if using).

4.  Refrigerate leftovers in an airtight container for up to 4 days. Shirataki rice doesn't freeze and thaw well, so this soup is best eaten fresh.

Macronutrients: Fat: 66%; Protein: 27%; Carbs: 7%

Per serving: Calories: 384; Total fat: 28g; Total carbs: 7g; Net carbs: 6g; Fiber: 1g; Protein: 26g

# LASAGNA SOUP

› SERVES 6

› **PREP TIME:** 10 MINUTES
› **COOK TIME:** 40 MINUTES

Who doesn't love lasagna? This soup version of the classic casserole is way easier to make, and it's all done in one pot, so there's far less to clean up. The trick to this recipe is letting it simmer to bring out all the wonderful flavors.

1 tablespoon avocado or olive oil

1 pound lean ground beef

½ cup diced yellow onion

1 garlic clove, minced

4 cups Chicken Bone Broth (page 26) or store-bought chicken broth

1 (14.5-ounce) can diced tomatoes

1 (14.5-ounce) can crushed tomatoes

1 tablespoon Italian seasoning

1 cup ricotta cheese

½ cup shredded mozzarella cheese

1 teaspoon pink Himalayan salt

Freshly ground black pepper

1 (14-ounce) can Palmini lasagna noodles, drained, rinsed, and chopped into spoon-size pieces

1. In a large soup pot, heat the oil over medium-high heat until it is shimmering. Add the ground beef and cook for about 8 minutes, until browned.

2. Add the onion and cook for about 4 minutes, until translucent. Add the garlic and cook for 1 additional minute, or until fragrant.

3. Spoon out and discard any fat, then add the broth, diced tomatoes and their juices, crushed tomatoes and their juices, and Italian seasoning. Turn the heat to high and bring the mixture to a boil. Then, reduce the heat to low and let the soup simmer, covered, for about 15 minutes.

4. Meanwhile, in a small bowl, mix the ricotta and mozzarella cheeses and set aside.

5. Add the salt and season with pepper, then stir in the Palmini noodles. Bring the soup back to a boil, then turn off the heat.

6. Divide the soup into bowls and top each with a dollop of the ricotta-mozzarella mixture. This will melt into the soup, adding oodles of cheesy flavor.

7. Refrigerate leftovers in an airtight container for up to 4 days or freeze for up to 3 months. Store the ricotta-mozzarella mixture separately from the soup.

Macronutrients: Fat: 49%; Protein: 38%; Carbs: 13%

Per serving: Calories: 338; Total fat: 18g; Total carbs: 13g; Net carbs: 10g; Fiber: 3g; Protein: 31g

# BEEF NOODLE SOUP

› SERVES 6
› DAIRY-FREE

› **PREP TIME:** 10 MINUTES
› **COOK TIME:** 1 HOUR
   20 MINUTES

Loaded with big, beefy flavors and plenty of veggies, this hearty soup is a satisfying and inexpensive meal when you use a tougher cut of meat like blade steaks or chuck roast. Cook it low and slow to tenderize the beef, and the flavors will be incredible. Use shirataki noodles to add miles of noodles to this flavor-packed dish without upping the carb count.

2 cups cubed beef (blade steak or chuck)

2 teaspoons pink Himalayan salt, divided

2 tablespoons avocado or olive oil, divided

½ cup diced yellow onion

½ cup diced celery

½ cup diced carrot

1 garlic clove, minced

6 cups Beef Bone Broth (page 27) or store-bought beef broth

1 (14.5-ounce) can diced tomatoes

½ teaspoon dried thyme

1 bay leaf

8 ounces white mushrooms, quartered

2 cups shirataki noodles, drained and well rinsed

Freshly ground black pepper

1. Season the beef cubes with 1 teaspoon of salt. In a large pot, heat 1 tablespoon of oil over medium-high heat and, working in batches, brown the beef until it is caramelized on all sides, 2 to 3 minutes per side. Set the beef aside.

2. In the same pot, heat the remaining 1 tablespoon of oil over medium-high heat and add the onion, celery, and carrot. Cook for 4 to 5 minutes, stirring frequently, or until the vegetables are soft and translucent. Add the garlic and cook for 1 additional minute.

3. Add the broth, tomatoes and their juices, thyme, bay leaf, and beef cubes and any accumulated juices to the pot with the vegetables. Bring to a boil, then turn down the heat to low and simmer for about 30 minutes, or until the beef cubes are tender.

4. Add the mushrooms and simmer for an additional 10 minutes, covered.

5. Remove the lid, add the shirataki noodles, and return the soup to a gentle boil over medium-high heat to heat the noodles through. Add the remaining 1 teaspoon of salt and season with pepper. Turn off the heat and serve.

6. Refrigerate leftovers in an airtight container for up to 4 days. Shirataki noodles don't freeze and thaw well, so this soup is best eaten fresh.

Other kinds of mushrooms will subtly change the flavor of this soup. Try it with cremini mushrooms, portobello mushrooms (remove the black gills), or even shiitake mushrooms.

Macronutrients: Fat: 51%; Protein: 35%; Carbs: 14%
Per serving: Calories: 195; Total fat: 11g; Total carbs: 7g; Net carbs: 5g; Fiber: 2g; Protein: 17g

# MEATBALL AND NOODLE SOUP

› SERVES 6  › **PREP TIME:** 10 MINUTES
 › **COOK TIME:** 30 MINUTES

With a rich, savory broth and miles of noodles along with tender meatballs, this soup version of the classic is hearty and satisfying. Shirataki noodles are a great keto choice, and you can indulge in this amazing soup for lunch or dinner, or even a tasty snack.

**For the meatballs**

Nonstick cooking spray

1 pound lean ground beef

1 large egg

1 tablespoon Italian seasoning

½ teaspoon pink Himalayan salt

**For the soup**

1 tablespoon avocado or olive oil

½ cup diced yellow onion

1 garlic clove, minced

4 cups Chicken Bone Broth (page 26) or store-bought chicken broth

1 (28-ounce) can plain tomato sauce

1 tablespoon Italian seasoning

1 (8-ounce) package shirataki spaghetti-style noodles, drained and rinsed

1 teaspoon pink Himalayan salt

½ cup grated Parmesan cheese

**To make the meatballs**

1. Preheat the oven to 350°F. Spray a baking sheet with cooking spray and set aside.

2. In a medium bowl, using your hands or a large wooden spoon, mix the ground beef with the egg, Italian seasoning, and salt. Form the meat into about 24 meatballs, each about 1½ inches in diameter.

3. Place the meatballs on the prepared baking sheet and bake for 15 minutes, or until cooked through and no longer pink in the middle. Set the meatballs aside until they're ready to go into the soup.

**To make the soup**

4. In a large pot, heat the oil over medium-high heat. Add the onion and cook for 4 to 5 minutes, stirring frequently, until it is soft and translucent. Add the garlic and cook for 1 additional minute, or until fragrant.

5. Add the broth, tomato sauce, and Italian seasoning to the pot. Cover and reduce the heat to low. Simmer for 15 minutes.

6. Gently lower the meatballs into the soup, cover, and cook for an additional 10 minutes.

7. Add the shirataki spaghetti-style noodles and salt, turn the heat to high, and bring the soup back to a boil to heat the noodles through. Turn off the heat.

8. Divide the soup between bowls and evenly sprinkle the Parmesan on top of each serving.

9. Refrigerate leftovers in an airtight container for up to 4 days. Shirataki noodles don't freeze well, so this soup is best eaten fresh.

## TIP

Zucchini noodles (zoodles) or even cooked spaghetti squash can be used in this soup instead of the shirataki noodles.

Macronutrients: Fat: 45%; Protein: 40%; Carbs: 15%

Per serving: Calories: 282; Total fat: 14g; Total carbs: 11g; Net carbs: 9g; Fiber: 2g; Protein: 28g

# EASY HERBED
# TOMATO BISQUE

Page 66

62

# 4

# Creamy Bisques and Chowders

# AVOCADO GAZPACHO

› SERVES 4
› VEGETARIAN

› **PREP TIME:** 15 MINUTES,
 PLUS 1 TO 2 HOURS
 TO CHILL

Gazpacho is the classic cold soup of Southern Spain. Traditional gazpacho uses day-old bread as its base to give the soup a great texture. This version uses the creaminess of pureed avocado rather than bread to create a creamy and hearty soup that's full of flavor and nutrition without gluten or excess carbohydrates. It works well as a starter course, a light lunch, or even an on-the-go savory breakfast smoothie. The acid from the lime will help slow the browning of the avocado, but this soup should still be eaten within 1 to 2 days.

2 cups chopped tomatoes

2 large ripe avocados, peeled and pitted

1 large cucumber, peeled and seeded

1 medium bell pepper (red, orange, or yellow), chopped

1 cup plain whole milk Greek yogurt

¼ cup avocado or olive oil

¼ cup chopped fresh cilantro

¼ cup chopped scallions, green part only

2 tablespoons red wine vinegar

Juice of 2 limes or 1 lemon

½ to 1 teaspoon pink Himalayan salt

¼ teaspoon freshly ground black pepper

1. In a blender, or in a large bowl if using an immersion blender, combine the tomatoes, avocados, cucumber, bell pepper, yogurt, oil, cilantro, scallions, vinegar, and lime juice. Blend until smooth. If using a stand blender, you may need to blend in two or three batches.

2. Add the salt and pepper and blend to combine the flavors.

3. Chill in the refrigerator for 1 to 2 hours before serving. Serve cold.

4. Refrigerate leftovers in an airtight container for 1 to 2 days.

Macronutrients: Fat: 74%; Protein: 7%; Carbs: 19%

Per serving: Calories: 383; Total fat: 31g; Total carbs: 20g; Net carbs: 11g; Fiber: 9g; Protein: 6g

# TOMATO–COCONUT CREAM BISQUE

› SERVES 4
› DAIRY-FREE, VEGAN

› **PREP TIME:** 10 MINUTES
› **COOK TIME:** 40 MINUTES

Roasting the tomatoes, onion, and garlic in the oven amps up the flavor, and coconut cream provides luxurious creaminess in this classic simple soup. Tomatoes are rich in the antioxidant lycopene, which gives them their bright-red color and is associated with a decreased risk of chronic disease.

Nonstick cooking spray

1 pound ripe cherry or grape tomatoes, coarsely chopped

1 yellow onion, coarsely chopped

2 garlic cloves, coarsely chopped

¼ cup avocado or olive oil, plus more for drizzling

2 thyme sprigs

Sea salt

Freshly ground black pepper

1 lemon, halved

1 cup coconut cream

⅓ cup chopped fresh basil

1. Preheat the oven to 400°F. Grease a baking dish with cooking spray and set aside.

2. Combine the tomatoes, onion, and garlic in the baking dish. Drizzle with the oil and toss in the thyme. Season with salt and pepper. Top with the lemon halves and roast for 20 minutes or until the tomatoes start to blister.

3. Remove the baking dish from the oven and transfer the mixture to a large saucepan over low heat. Stir in the coconut cream and bring the soup to a simmer. Cook for 20 minutes to allow the flavors to meld.

4. Remove and discard the lemon halves. Turn off the heat and blend the soup with an immersion blender until it is silky smooth (adding warm water if necessary to reach the desired texture).

5. Finish with a drizzle of oil and the basil, and season with additional salt and pepper, if desired.

6. Refrigerate leftovers in an airtight container for up to 4 days.

Macronutrients: Fat: 84%; Protein: 3%; Carbs: 13%
Per serving: Calories: 356; Total fat: 35g; Total carbs: 12g; Net carbs: 9g; Fiber: 3g; Protein: 4g

# EASY HERBED TOMATO BISQUE

> SERVES 8

> **PREP TIME:** 15 MINUTES
> **COOK TIME:** 25 MINUTES

Just the thought of warm tomato soup and low-carb grilled cheese made on keto-friendly bread brings a smile to my face. This flavorful tomato bisque is so easy, creamy, and delicious. Try serving it with Cheesy Garlic Rolls (page 105), which are to die for. I prefer using San Marzano style canned whole tomatoes for this recipe.

3 tablespoons avocado or olive oil

½ cup diced yellow onion

2 garlic cloves, coarsely chopped

1 (28-ounce) can whole tomatoes

1 cup Chicken Bone Broth (page 26) or store-bought chicken broth

1 tablespoon tomato paste

½ teaspoon dried basil

½ teaspoon dried thyme

1 tablespoon freshly squeezed lemon juice

½ cup heavy (whipping) cream

1. In a large pot or Dutch oven, heat the oil over medium heat. Sauté the onion for about 5 minutes, until the onion is translucent but not brown. Add the garlic and cook for 1 minute more.

2. Stir in the tomatoes and their juices, broth, tomato paste, basil, and thyme, stirring to break up the chunks of tomato. Reduce the heat to low and simmer for 15 to 20 minutes.

3. Use an immersion blender to blend the soup until smooth, or carefully transfer the soup to a blender and blend until smooth. Use caution while blending hot liquids and cover the blender lid with a towel. Pour the soup back into the pot. Stir in the lemon juice and cream.

4. Serve hot.

5. Refrigerate leftovers in an airtight container for up to 4 days.

Macronutrients: Fat: 76%; Protein: 5%; Carbs: 19%

Per serving: Calories: 132; Total fat: 11g; Total carbs: 7g; Net carbs: 5g; Fiber: 2g; Protein: 2g

# CAULIFLOWER-CHEDDAR SOUP

› SERVES 8

› **PREP TIME:** 10 MINUTES
› **COOK TIME:** 30 MINUTES

Cauliflower is a versatile vegetable that can be eaten on the keto diet in many recipes, such as this creamy soup. Cauliflower is an excellent source of vitamins C and K, omega-3 fatty acids, and manganese, which can help support digestion, improve brain function, and promote a healthy heart. Choose a snowy-white head of cauliflower with crisp green leaves and absolutely no brown spots.

4 tablespoons (½ stick) unsalted butter

1 head cauliflower, chopped

½ cup diced yellow onion

4 cups Chicken Bone Broth (page 26) or store-bought chicken broth

½ teaspoon ground nutmeg

1 cup heavy (whipping) cream

Sea salt

Freshly ground black pepper

1 cup shredded cheddar cheese

1. In a large stockpot, melt the butter over medium heat.

2. Sauté the cauliflower and onion for about 10 minutes, until tender and lightly browned.

3. Add the broth and nutmeg to the pot and bring the liquid to a boil. Reduce the heat to low and simmer until the vegetables are very tender, about 15 minutes.

4. Remove the pot from the heat, stir in the cream, and puree the soup with an immersion blender or a food processor until smooth.

5. Season the soup with salt and pepper and serve topped with the cheddar cheese.

6. Refrigerate leftovers in an airtight container for up to 4 days or freeze for up to 3 months.

Macronutrients: Fat: 77%; Protein: 16%; Carbs: 7%

Per serving: Calories: 245; Total fat: 21g; Total carbs: 4g; Net carbs: 3g; Fiber: 1g; Protein: 10g

# CREAM OF CAULIFLOWER GAZPACHO

› SERVES 4 TO 6
› DAIRY-FREE

› **PREP TIME:** 15 MINUTES
› **COOK TIME:** 30 MINUTES

Each region in Spain has its favorite style of gazpacho, a traditional cold soup. A creamy white version using almonds, garlic, and leftover bread is popular in Malaga, a port city in Southern Spain with rich culinary influences from North Africa. My version substitutes cauliflower for the bread, can be served warm or cold, and is rich with the flavor that defines the cuisine of the region. Blanching the almonds and removing the skin creates a silky-smooth texture. In Spain, Marcona almonds, blanched almonds tossed in olive oil and salt, are a common snack. You can find them at gourmet grocery stores in the United States, but they are typically pricey, so try making your own as outlined here.

1 cup raw almonds

½ teaspoon pink Himalayan salt

½ cup avocado or olive oil, plus 1 tablespoon, divided

1 small white onion, diced

1 small head cauliflower, stalk removed and broken into florets (about 3 cups)

2 garlic cloves, finely minced

2 cups Chicken Bone Broth (page 26) or store-bought vegetable stock or chicken broth, plus more if needed

1 tablespoon red wine vinegar

¼ teaspoon freshly ground black pepper

1. Bring a small pot of water to a boil. Add the almonds to the water and boil for 1 minute, being careful to not boil longer or else the almonds will become soggy. Drain the almonds in a colander and run under cold water. Pat dry and, using your fingers, squeeze each almond out of its skin. Discard the skins.

2. In a food processor or blender, blend together the almonds and salt. With the processor running, drizzle in ½ cup of oil, scraping down the sides as needed. Set the almond paste aside.

3. In a large stockpot, heat the remaining 1 tablespoon of oil over medium-high heat. Add the onion and sauté for 3 to 4 minutes, until golden. Add the cauliflower florets and sauté for another 3 to 4 minutes. Add the garlic and sauté for 1 minute more, until fragrant.

4. Add the broth and bring to a boil. Cover, reduce the heat to medium-low, and simmer for 8 to 10 minutes until tender. Remove from the heat and allow to cool slightly.

5. Add the vinegar and pepper. Using an immersion blender, blend until smooth. Alternatively, you can use a stand blender, but you may need to divide the mixture into two or three batches. With the blender running, add the almond paste and blend until smooth, adding extra broth if the soup is too thick.

6. Serve warm or chill in the refrigerator for at least 4 to 6 hours to serve cold.

7. Refrigerate leftovers in an airtight container for up to 4 days or freeze for up to 3 months.

## TIP

For ease, you can substitute prepared almond butter for the blanched almonds, but it will have more of a fibrous texture due to the skins in the almond butter.

Macronutrients: Fat: 80%; Protein: 11%; Carbs: 9%
Per serving: Calories: 545; Total fat: 48g; Total carbs: 15g; Net carbs: 9g; Fiber: 6g; Protein: 15g

# BROCCOLI CHEDDAR SOUP

› SERVES 4

› **PREP TIME:** 10 MINUTES
› **COOK TIME:** 20 MINUTES

A lot of soups like this one usually start with butter and flour to thicken them, but skipping the flour really doesn't make a difference, especially if you use heavy cream instead of regular milk. This soup is warm, nourishing, and keto-friendly.

4 tablespoons (½ stick) unsalted butter

1 celery stalk, diced

1 carrot, diced

½ yellow onion, diced

1 garlic clove, minced

3 cups Chicken Bone Broth (page 26) or store-bought chicken broth

2 cups broccoli florets

1 cup heavy (whipping) cream

2½ cups shredded cheddar cheese

Pink Himalayan salt

Freshly ground black pepper

1. In a large saucepan, melt the butter over medium heat. Add the celery, carrot, onion, and garlic. Stir to combine and sauté for 5 to 7 minutes until softened.

2. Stir in the chicken broth and bring to a simmer.

3. Add the broccoli. Simmer for 5 to 7 minutes, then add the cream. Turn the heat up to medium-high and bring the soup back to a simmer. Turn off the heat.

4. While stirring, slowly add the cheese, letting it melt completely. Don't boil the soup once you've added the cheese because the cheese could break and curdle. If the cheese isn't melting, turn the heat on low and stir frequently until it has all melted. Season well with salt and pepper and serve hot.

5. Refrigerate leftovers in an airtight container for up to 5 days.

## TIP

Top each serving with 2 crumbled pieces of cooked bacon and some sliced scallions.

Macronutrients: Fat: 75%; Protein: 20%; Carbs: 5%

Per serving: Calories: 655; Total fat: 55g; Total carbs: 11g; Net carbs: 9g; Fiber: 2g; Protein: 30g

# LOADED BAKED "FAUXTATO" SOUP

› SERVES 6

› **PREP TIME:** 15 MINUTES
› **COOK TIME:** 20 MINUTES

This loaded baked "fauxtato" soup will warm your keto soul when the temperature dips down. It's simple to make and is so luscious that you won't want to put down your spoon.

3 tablespoons unsalted butter

1¼ pounds turnips (about 5), peeled and diced into 1-inch cubes

¼ cup chopped yellow onion

1 teaspoon pink Himalayan salt

½ teaspoon garlic powder

12 ounces cauliflower florets, fresh or frozen, steamed until just tender

2½ to 3 cups Chicken Bone Broth (page 26) or store-bought chicken broth, plus more as needed

⅓ cup heavy (whipping) cream

2 tablespoons sour cream

Freshly ground black pepper

Crispy cooked bacon, chopped, for garnish (optional)

Shredded cheddar cheese, for garnish (optional)

Sliced scallion, for garnish (optional)

1. In a medium saucepan, melt the butter over medium heat. Add the turnips, onion, salt, and garlic powder. Sauté for 8 to 10 minutes, until the onion is tender and the turnips begin to pick up some golden-brown color.

2. Add the cauliflower and cook for 1 to 2 minutes more.

3. Add the broth and bring the mixture to a boil. Lower the heat to maintain a simmer and cook for 7 to 8 minutes, or until the turnips are fork-tender. Remove from the heat and let cool for a few minutes.

4. Carefully pour the soup into a blender. Add the heavy cream and sour cream. Blend on high speed until smooth and creamy. (Alternatively, use an immersion blender in the pot.) Adjust the consistency with additional broth and season with pepper and salt, as needed.

5. Serve topped with bacon, cheese, and scallion (if using).

6. Refrigerate leftovers in an airtight container for up to 4 days or freeze for up to 3 months.

Macronutrients: Fat: 62%; Protein: 9%; Carbs: 29%

Per serving: Calories: 184; Total fat: 13g; Total carbs: 13g; Net carbs: 10g; Fiber: 3g; Protein: 5g

# CREAM OF ASPARAGUS SOUP

› SERVES 4

› **PREP TIME:** 10 MINUTES
› **COOK TIME:** 35 MINUTES

With a delicate asparagus flavor and a hint of lemon, this amazing soup is so creamy and delightful that you'll be going back for more.

1 tablespoon pink Himalayan salt, plus ½ teaspoon, divided

2 pounds asparagus, trimmed, divided

2 tablespoons salted butter

½ cup diced yellow onion

½ cup diced celery

5 cups Chicken Bone Broth (page 26) or store-bought chicken broth

1 tablespoon freshly squeezed lemon juice

1 cup heavy (whipping) cream

½ teaspoon xanthan gum (optional)

¼ teaspoon freshly ground black pepper

1. Fill a medium soup pot halfway with water, add 1 tablespoon of salt, and bring to a boil over high heat. Add 3 spears of asparagus and boil for 1 minute. Remove the asparagus and run them under cold water to stop the cooking. Chop this asparagus and set it aside for the garnish.

2. Dry out the pot and return it to the stove. Melt the butter over medium-high heat and add the onion and celery. Sauté for about 5 minutes, until the onion and celery are soft.

3. Add the broth and bring to a boil over high heat. Add the remaining uncooked asparagus and reduce the heat to low. Simmer for 15 minutes, or until the asparagus is quite soft.

4. Working in batches, carefully transfer the soup to a blender. Place a towel over the top and hold down the lid, then pulse the mixture until smooth. (Alternatively, use an immersion blender to puree the soup in the pot.)

5. Return the soup to the pot and bring it back to a boil. Then turn off the heat. Stir in the lemon juice and then the cream, stirring well to combine.

6. To thicken, whisk in the xanthan gum (if using). Add the remaining ½ teaspoon of salt and the pepper. Garnish each bowl evenly with the reserved chopped asparagus and serve.

7. Refrigerate leftovers in an airtight container for up to 3 days or freeze for up to 3 months.

### TIP

Save time by using frozen asparagus in this recipe. Simply thaw and drain the asparagus before using it and proceed with the recipe as written. If you use fresh asparagus, be sure to clean it very well under running water to remove any sand or grit.

Macronutrients: Fat: 67%; Protein: 18%; Carbs: 15%

Per serving: Calories: 376; Total fat: 28g; Total carbs: 14g; Net carbs: 9g; Fiber: 5g; Protein: 17g

# CREAM OF MUSHROOM SOUP

› SERVES 4

› **PREP TIME:** 10 MINUTES
› **COOK TIME:** 30 MINUTES

A creamy broth and loads of savory mushroom flavor infuse this soup. A little different from other mushroom soups, this one includes both pureed mushrooms and sliced mushrooms, ensuring plenty of texture that's delicious to the last spoonful.

3 tablespoons salted butter, divided

1 pound white or brown mushrooms, trimmed and sliced

½ cup diced yellow onion

½ cup diced celery

2 garlic cloves, minced

4 cups Chicken Bone Broth (page 26) or store-bought chicken broth

½ teaspoon dried thyme

1 cup heavy (whipping) cream

½ teaspoon pink Himalayan salt

¼ teaspoon freshly ground black pepper

2 tablespoons chopped fresh chives

1. In a medium pot, melt 1 tablespoon of butter over medium-high heat. Add the mushrooms and cook for 5 to 6 minutes, until they've given off all their liquid. Remove about half of the mushrooms and set them aside.

2. Add the remaining 2 tablespoons of butter to the pot and add the onion, celery, and garlic and sauté for 4 to 5 minutes, until the onions and celery are soft.

3. Add the broth and thyme to the pot. Bring the soup to a boil over medium-high heat, then reduce the heat to low and simmer for about 15 minutes.

4. Turn off the heat, add the cream, and mix well. Working in batches, transfer the mixture to a blender. Cover the top of the blender with a towel and, holding the lid down tightly, pulse to puree. (Alternatively, use an immersion blender to puree the mixture in the pot.)

5. Pour the pureed soup back into the pot and add the reserved sliced mushrooms. Heat the soup through, without boiling, and add the salt and pepper. Garnish each bowl with 1½ teaspoons of chopped chives before serving.

6. Refrigerate leftovers in an airtight container for up to 4 days or freeze for up to 3 months.

Macronutrients: Fat: 74%; Protein: 16%; Carbs: 10%

Per serving: Calories: 375; Total fat: 31g; Total carbs: 9g; Net carbs: 7g; Fiber: 2g; Protein: 15g

# MANHATTAN CLAM CHOWDER

› SERVES 6
› DAIRY-FREE

› **PREP TIME:** 10 MINUTES
› **COOK TIME:** 30 MINUTES

Clam chowders come in two styles: brothy or creamy. This brothy chowder is loaded with tasty veggies and succulent clams. With a rich broth, it's oh so scoopable and delicious.

1 tablespoon avocado or olive oil

½ cup diced yellow onion

2 slices bacon, chopped

2 garlic cloves, minced

4 cups clam juice

1 (28-ounce) can diced tomatoes

2 cups Chicken Bone Broth (page 26) or store-bought chicken broth

¼ cup tomato paste

½ teaspoon dried thyme

2 cups minced clams

1 teaspoon pink Himalayan salt

Freshly ground black pepper

1. In a large pot, heat the oil over medium heat until it is shimmering. Add the onion and bacon and cook for about 5 minutes, until the onion is translucent.

2. Add the garlic and cook for 1 additional minute, until fragrant.

3. Add the clam juice, diced tomatoes and their juices, broth, tomato paste, and thyme and bring to a boil over high heat. Reduce the heat to low, cover the pot, and simmer the broth for 15 minutes.

4. Add the minced clams to the broth and simmer for another 5 minutes. Add the salt and season with pepper. Serve warm.

5. Refrigerate leftovers in an airtight container for up to 3 days or freeze for up to 3 months.

## TIP

You can use canned clams for convenience, but you can also use fresh clams. Rinse the clam meat well under running water and coarsely chop it. Allow the clam meat to cook for an additional minute in the hot broth until it's fully cooked.

Macronutrients: Fat: 30%; Protein: 44%; Carbs: 26%

Per serving: Calories: 182; Total fat: 6g; Total carbs: 12g; Net carbs: 9g; Fiber: 3g; Protein: 20g

# CHICKEN AND CHIPOTLE CHOWDER

› SERVES 6

› **PREP TIME:** 10 MINUTES
› **COOK TIME:** 25 MINUTES

This thick, chunky, and slightly spicy soup is going to knock your socks off. I've been making this soup for decades, and my secret ingredient to this fantastic chowder is chipotle powder. Once a specialty product, it's now widely available in the spice section of most grocery stores. It's the perfect smoky and spicy addition to this soup. Add a little or a lot; it's up to you.

2 slices bacon, chopped

½ cup diced yellow onion

½ cup diced celery

1 garlic clove, minced

4 cups Chicken Bone Broth (page 26) or store-bought chicken broth

2 cups chopped cooked chicken

1 cup heavy (whipping) cream

½ teaspoon chipotle powder

1 teaspoon pink Himalayan salt

¼ teaspoon freshly ground black pepper

½ teaspoon xanthan gum (optional)

1. In a medium skillet, fry the bacon over medium-high heat for about 4 minutes, until crisp. Remove the bacon from the pan, reserving the bacon fat in the pan. Set the bacon aside to use as a garnish.

2. Add the onion, celery, and garlic to the same skillet with the reserved bacon fat and sauté for 4 to 5 minutes, until the onion and celery are soft.

3. Transfer the vegetable mixture to a large pot and add the broth and cooked chicken. Bring to a boil over high heat. Then reduce the heat to low and simmer for about 10 minutes.

4. Turn off the heat and add the cream and chipotle powder. Stir until well combined, then add the salt and pepper. To thicken, whisk in the xanthan gum (if using). Divide the soup into bowls and garnish with the reserved crispy bacon before serving.

5. Refrigerate leftovers in an airtight container for up to 4 days or freeze for up to 3 months. Store the bacon separately, then re-crisp it in a small skillet or in the microwave on high power for about 20 seconds.

Macronutrients: Fat: 63%; Protein: 32%; Carbs: 5%

Per serving: Calories: 288; Total fat: 20g; Total carbs: 4g; Net carbs: 4g; Fiber: 0g; Protein: 23g

# HAM AND CHEDDAR CHOWDER

› SERVES 6      › **PREP TIME:** 10 MINUTES
              › **COOK TIME:** 35 MINUTES

Ham and cheese are a classic combination, and this delicious soup is rich, creamy, and loaded with flavor. The big chunks of ham make this a hearty soup that's perfect as a meal or as part of a meal.

2 slices bacon, chopped

½ cup diced yellow onion

½ cup diced celery

1 garlic clove, minced

5 cups Chicken Bone Broth (page 26) or store-bought chicken broth

½ teaspoon dried thyme

2 cups diced ham

1 cup shredded sharp cheddar cheese

1 cup heavy (whipping) cream

¼ teaspoon freshly ground black pepper

½ teaspoon xanthan gum (optional)

1. In a medium skillet, fry the bacon over medium-high heat for about 4 minutes, until crisp. Remove the bacon, reserving the bacon fat in the pan, and set aside.

2. Add the onion, celery, and garlic to the same skillet with the reserved bacon fat and sauté for 4 to 5 minutes, until the onion and celery are soft. Transfer the vegetables to a large soup pot.

3. Add the broth and thyme to the soup pot and bring to a boil over medium-high heat. Then reduce the heat to low and simmer for about 10 minutes.

4. Add the ham and bring the soup back to a boil on medium-high heat. Then lower the heat and simmer for an additional 10 minutes.

5. Turn off the heat and add the cheese, stirring well until it is all melted into the soup. Add the cream and mix well. Turn the heat back on low for a few minutes just to heat the soup through, but don't boil it. Add the pepper. To thicken, whisk in the xanthan gum (if using). Serve warm.

6. Refrigerate leftovers in an airtight container for up to 4 days or freeze for up to 3 months.

Macronutrients: Fat: 64%; Protein: 28%; Carbs: 8%

Per serving: Calories: 366; Total fat: 26g; Total carbs: 7g; Net carbs: 7g; Fiber: 0g; Protein: 26g

# BACON AND SHRIMP CHOWDER

› SERVES 6

› **PREP TIME:** 10 MINUTES
› **COOK TIME:** 20 MINUTES

Smoky bacon pairs deliciously with sweet and tender shrimp in this fully loaded chowder. It's creamy and chunky and complements a salad or your favorite chaffle sandwich. You should use medium-size shrimp in this recipe, but if your shrimp are larger, feel free to chop them or, for a prettier presentation, butterfly the shrimp and cut them all the way through. They'll curl up when cooking.

6 slices bacon, chopped

½ cup diced yellow onion

½ cup diced celery

½ cup diced carrot

1 garlic clove, minced

6 cups Chicken Bone Broth (page 26) or store-bought chicken broth

½ teaspoon dried thyme

1 pound shrimp, shelled and deveined

1 cup heavy (whipping) cream

1 teaspoon pink Himalayan salt

Freshly ground black pepper

¼ teaspoon xanthan gum (optional)

1. In a large pot, fry the bacon over medium-high heat for about 4 minutes, until crispy. Remove the bacon from the pan and set aside, reserving the bacon fat in the pan.

2. Add the onion, celery, and carrot to the bacon fat and cook for 4 to 5 minutes, until the onion is translucent. Spoon out most of the fat, leaving the vegetables behind. Add the garlic and cook for 1 additional minute, or until fragrant.

3. Add the broth and thyme and simmer, covered, for 10 minutes.

4. Add the shrimp and simmer for 1 or 2 minutes, or until the shrimp are pink, opaque, and slightly curled up.

5. Add the cream and salt to the soup and season with pepper. Stir well to incorporate. To thicken, whisk in the xanthan gum (if using).

6. Divide into bowls and garnish with some of the crispy bacon before serving.

7. Refrigerate leftovers in an airtight container for up to 3 days or freeze for up to 3 months. Package the bacon separately, then re-crisp it in a small skillet or in the microwave on high power for about 20 seconds.

Macronutrients: Fat: 62%; Protein: 33%; Carbs: 5%

Per serving: Calories: 365; Total fat: 25g; Total carbs: 5g; Net carbs: 4g; Fiber: 1g; Protein: 30g

# SALMON AND ZUCCHINI CHOWDER

› SERVES 6

› **PREP TIME:** 15 MINUTES
› **COOK TIME:** 40 MINUTES

This chowder is a rich and savory twist on classic chowders. The sweet and light flavor of fresh salmon pairs beautifully with zucchini in this hearty chowder that's always a great pick on a cold day.

2 slices bacon, chopped

½ cup diced yellow onion

½ cup diced celery

1 garlic clove, minced

4 cups Chicken Bone Broth (page 26) or store-bought chicken broth

½ teaspoon dried thyme

2 cups diced zucchini

8 ounces fresh salmon fillets, pin bones and skin removed

1 cup heavy (whipping) cream

1 teaspoon pink Himalayan salt

¼ teaspoon freshly ground black pepper

½ teaspoon xanthan gum (optional)

1. In a medium skillet, fry the bacon over medium-high heat for about 4 minutes, until crisp. Remove from the pan and set aside, reserving the bacon fat in the pan.

2. Add the onion, celery, and garlic to the reserved bacon fat and sauté for 4 to 5 minutes, until the onion and celery are soft. Transfer the vegetables to a large pot.

3. Add the broth and thyme to the pot. Bring to a boil over medium-high heat, then reduce the heat to low and simmer for about 10 minutes.

4. Add the zucchini and bring the pot back to a boil over medium-high heat. Lower the heat and simmer for an additional 2 minutes.

5. Meanwhile, in the same skillet, cook the salmon in the residual bacon fat. Add the oil (if using) if your pan is too dry. Cook the salmon over low heat for 6 to 8 minutes, or until it is opaque and cooked in the center. Set aside.

6. Turn off the heat, add the salmon, breaking it up into spoon-size chunks, and stir in the cream. Stir until well combined and add the salt and pepper. To thicken, whisk in the xanthan gum (if using). Divide into bowls and garnish with the reserved bacon before serving.

Macronutrients: Fat: 67%; Protein: 26%; Carbs: 7%

Per serving: Calories: 281; Total fat: 21g; Total carbs: 5g; Net carbs: 4g; Fiber: 1g; Protein: 18g

# CHICKEN POTPIE SOUP

› SERVES 6

› **PREP TIME:** 10 MINUTES
› **COOK TIME:** 35 MINUTES

Loaded with big chunks of tender vegetables and chicken, chicken potpie soup is a guilt-free way to enjoy all the flavors of the homey dish without the carbs. There are peas in this recipe, which you can skip if you're doing strict keto.

2 tablespoons salted butter

1 cup sliced carrots

½ cup diced yellow onion

½ cup diced celery

1 garlic clove, minced

1 pound boneless, skinless chicken breast, cut into ½-inch pieces

4 cups Chicken Bone Broth (page 26) or store-bought chicken broth

½ cup fresh or frozen peas

2 cups heavy (whipping) cream

½ teaspoon pink Himalayan salt

¼ teaspoon freshly ground black pepper, plus more for garnish

½ teaspoon xanthan gum (optional)

2 tablespoons chopped fresh parsley

1. In a medium pot, melt the butter over low heat. Add the carrots, onion, celery, and garlic. Sauté for about 5 minutes, until the onions are soft.

2. Add the chicken to the vegetables and cook for 3 to 5 minutes over medium heat, until the chicken is no longer pink.

3. Add the broth and bring to a simmer. Cover the pot, reduce the heat to low, and simmer for 20 minutes.

4. Add the peas to the soup and bring the soup back to a boil. Then, turn off the heat and stir in the cream. You can heat the soup through, but be careful not to boil the cream.

5. Add the salt and pepper and thicken by whisking in the xanthan gum (if using).

6. Divide into bowls and top each with 1 teaspoon of chopped parsley and a few grinds of pepper to serve.

7. Refrigerate leftovers in an airtight container for up to 3 days or freeze for up to 3 months.

Macronutrients: Fat: 68%; Protein: 24%; Carbs: 8%

Per serving: Calories: 463; Total fat: 35g; Total carbs: 9g; Net carbs: 7g; Fiber: 2g; Protein: 28g

**TOM YUM SOUP**

Page 92

# 5

# Vegetarian and Veggie-Centric Soups

# HEARTY CAULIFLOWER SOUP

› SERVES 4      › **PREP TIME:** 10 MINUTES
     › **COOK TIME:** 1 HOUR

Creamy, hearty soups fill the belly and warm the heart. By using low-carb cauliflower, buttery mascarpone cheese, and heavy cream, this soup is everything a keto comfort soup should be. Mascarpone is best for its richness, but you can also use full-fat cream cheese. No bone broth? Simply use low-sodium chicken broth. You really can't go wrong with this hearty soup.

4 cups cauliflower florets

4 tablespoons (½ stick) unsalted butter, melted

¼ teaspoon pink Himalayan salt, plus more for seasoning

1 tablespoon avocado or olive oil

1 garlic clove, minced

¼ cup diced yellow onion

Pinch ground nutmeg

⅛ teaspoon thyme

2 cups Chicken Bone Broth (page 26) or store-bought chicken broth

2 tablespoons mascarpone, at room temperature

¼ cup heavy (whipping) cream

Freshly ground black pepper

1. Preheat the oven to 375°F. Line a baking sheet with parchment paper and set aside.

2. In a large bowl, toss the cauliflower, butter, and salt together until well combined. Arrange the cauliflower on the prepared baking sheet in a single layer. Bake for 30 minutes, until the cauliflower is fork-tender and begins to brown.

3. In a large saucepan, heat the oil over medium-low heat. Add the garlic, stirring frequently, and cook for about 45 seconds. Stir in the onion, sprinkle in the nutmeg and thyme, and cook for another 5 to 7 minutes, until the onions are translucent.

4. Transfer the roasted cauliflower to the saucepan and stir together.

5. Add the broth and bring the soup to a boil over medium-high heat. Reduce the heat to medium-low and simmer for 15 to 20 minutes, until all the vegetables are soft.

6. Stir in the mascarpone ½ tablespoon at a time until melted. Slowly add the cream, stirring constantly, until it is thoroughly incorporated. Season with salt and pepper.

7. Transfer three-fourths of the soup to a blender and blend until smooth. Pour the blended soup back into the saucepan and stir to combine. This method uses the soup itself as a thickener.

8. Portion the soup into bowls and serve.

9. Refrigerate leftovers in an airtight container for up to 4 days or freeze for up to 3 months.

## TIP

Create a version of loaded baked potato soup by topping each bowl with a cooked, crumbled piece of bacon, 1 tablespoon of shredded cheddar cheese, 1½ teaspoons of sour cream, and 1 teaspoon of chopped scallion.

Macronutrients: Fat: 70%; Protein: 19%; Carbs: 11%
Per serving: Calories: 256; Total fat: 20g; Total carbs: 8g; Net carbs: 6g; Fiber: 2g; Protein: 11g

# AVOCADO-LIME SOUP

‣ SERVES 4

‣ **PREP TIME:** 5 MINUTES
‣ **COOK TIME:** 30 MINUTES

This soup has a festive flair, making it the perfect lunchtime or dinnertime pick-me-up. Whether you are building an empire or planning your next epic nap, you need those omega-3 fatty acids, and this soup is chock-full of them.

2 tablespoons avocado or olive oil

½ yellow onion, chopped

1 teaspoon ground cumin

1 teaspoon ground coriander

1 teaspoon chili powder

1 cup chopped cabbage, divided

1 medium tomato, chopped

½ cup chopped fresh cilantro, plus more for garnish

½ cup chopped celery

¼ cup hemp hearts

½ jalapeño pepper, seeded and chopped

8 cups vegetable broth

Juice of 2 limes

1 avocado, peeled, pitted, and cut into cubes

3 Sesame Seed Crackers (page 100)

1. In a large stockpot, heat the oil over medium heat and add the onion, cumin, coriander, and chili powder. Sauté, stirring occasionally, for about 5 minutes, until the onion becomes tender.

2. Add ¾ cup of cabbage, the tomato, cilantro, celery, hemp hearts, and jalapeño to the pot. Stir to coat the spices and cook for 4 minutes.

3. Pour the broth into the pot and simmer on low for 20 minutes. Remove the pot from the heat and stir in the lime juice.

4. Divide the avocado equally between serving bowls. Pour the soup over the avocado in the bowls and garnish with the remaining ¼ cup of cabbage and cilantro.

5. Break the crackers over the top of the soup to create a "tortilla soup" vibe before serving.

6. Refrigerate leftovers in an airtight container for 1 to 2 days.

When shopping for the perfect avocado, it's important to test for ripeness. Hold the fruit in your hand and give it a gentle squeeze. If the avocado gives to your touch, it's ready to be eaten. If it's too firm, store it in a brown paper bag on the countertop for a day or so until the avocado has ripened.

Macronutrients: Fat: 64%; Protein: 19%; Carbs: 17%
Per serving: Calories: 168; Total fat: 12g; Total carbs: 7g; Net carbs: 3g; Fiber: 4g; Protein: 8g

# BUTTERNUT SQUASH SOUP WITH TURMERIC AND GINGER

> SERVES 8
> DAIRY-FREE, VEGAN

> **PREP TIME:** 10 MINUTES
> **COOK TIME:** 35 MINUTES

Nothing says cozy comfort more than an epic butternut squash soup. Lemongrass adds extra layers of flavor. The ginger and turmeric are anti-inflammatory and add warmth to this lovely and colorful soup.

1 small butternut squash

3 tablespoons coconut oil

3 shallots, coarsely chopped

1-inch knob fresh ginger, peeled and coarsely chopped

1-inch knob fresh turmeric root, peeled and coarsely chopped

1 fresh lemongrass stalk, coarsely chopped

½ cup dry marsala (optional)

8 cups vegetable broth

1 cup coconut cream

Cold-pressed olive oil, for drizzling

Handful toasted pumpkin seeds, for garnish (optional)

1. Preheat the oven to 365°F.

2. Puncture the squash skin with a fork several times to create air vents. Put the entire squash into a baking dish and bake for 30 minutes or until the squash is extremely tender.

3. While the squash is baking, in a large stockpot, heat the coconut oil over medium heat. Add the shallots, ginger, turmeric, and lemongrass to the pot and sauté until the spices become fragrant and the shallots are tender, about 5 minutes.

4. Deglaze the pot by pouring in the marsala (if using) and stirring, scraping the bottom of the pot to loosen any stuck bits. Simmer for 2 to 3 minutes to allow the alcohol to start to reduce. Then, add the broth and reduce the heat to low.

5. Remove the squash from the oven and poke it with a fork to check for tenderness. Carefully cut the squash in half lengthwise, allowing any liquid to drain out. Once the squash is cool enough to handle, scoop out the seeds. With a paring knife, remove the skin. Coarsely chop the squash and add it to the stockpot.

6. Pour the coconut cream into the pot, bring to a simmer, and remove from the heat.

7.  Using an immersion blender, blend the soup thoroughly until smooth and velvety. Alternatively, you can transfer the soup to a blender, pulse until smooth, and return the mixture to the pot. Drizzle with olive oil and top with toasted pumpkin seeds (if using). Serve warm.

8.  Refrigerate leftovers in an airtight container for up to 5 days.

## TIP

To make this a cold-busting soup, double the ginger, squeeze in 1 tablespoon of fresh lemon juice, and add a couple of handfuls of raw spinach after blending and allow it to wilt.

Macronutrients: Fat: 71%; Protein: 3%; Carbs: 26%
Per serving: Calories: 186; Total fat: 16g; Total carbs: 13g; Net carbs: 10g; Fiber: 3g; Protein: 2g

# WATERCRESS-SPINACH SOUP

› SERVES 4
› DAIRY-FREE

› **PREP TIME:** 10 MINUTES
› **COOK TIME:** 10 MINUTES

Watercress is a green that is often used in fine dining as both an ingredient and a lovely garnish. The peppery, subtle taste of this plant is perfect with the more assertive spinach in this gorgeous soup. As its name implies, watercress grows in water, so its freshness is best maintained after purchase by submerging it in a container of water in the refrigerator.

2 tablespoons coconut oil

½ yellow onion, chopped

2 teaspoons minced garlic

4 cups Chicken Bone Broth (page 26) or store-bought chicken broth

4 cups watercress

4 cups spinach

1 cup full-fat unsweetened coconut milk

Pink Himalayan salt

Freshly ground black pepper

½ teaspoon xanthan gum (optional)

8 cooked turkey bacon slices, chopped

1. In a large saucepan, heat the coconut oil over medium-high heat. Sauté the onion and garlic for about 3 minutes, until softened.

2. Add the broth, watercress, spinach, and coconut milk. Cook for about 3 minutes, until the mixture is just heated through and the greens are still vibrant.

3. Blend with an immersion blender, or transfer the soup to a food processor or blender, puree, and transfer the soup back to the saucepan. Season with salt and pepper.

4. To thicken, whisk in the xanthan gum (if using).

5. Divide the soup into bowls, top with the bacon, and serve.

6. Refrigerate leftovers in an airtight container for up to 5 days or freeze for up to 3 months.

Macronutrients: Fat: 65%; Protein: 25%; Carbs: 10%

Per serving: Calories: 310; Total fat: 22g; Total carbs: 9g; Net carbs: 8g; Fiber: 1g; Protein: 19g

# TUSCAN KALE SOUP

› SERVES 8
› DAIRY-FREE, VEGAN

› **PREP TIME:** 10 MINUTES
› **COOK TIME:** 35 MINUTES

Kale is one of the world's best sources of vitamin K and is also rich in iron and other anti-oxidants to help prevent aging and disease. Sneak kale into your meals whenever you get the chance.

2 tablespoons avocado or olive oil

½ cup finely diced yellow onion

2 garlic cloves, chopped

2 tablespoons dried oregano

8 cups vegetable broth

¼ cup hemp hearts

3 cups kale, destemmed and leaves cut into thin ribbons

1 cup chopped fresh parsley, plus a few sprigs for garnish

½ cup diced rutabaga

⅓ cup diced sun-dried tomatoes

⅓ cup diced carrot

Juice of 1 lemon

Sea salt

1. In a large stockpot, heat the oil over medium heat. Add the onion, garlic, and oregano and cook for about 5 minutes, stirring frequently to prevent sticking, until the onion is tender and the garlic is fragrant.

2. Pour the broth into the pot, turn the heat to low, and bring to a simmer. After the broth has been simmering for about 5 minutes, add the hemp hearts and simmer for another 15 minutes.

3. Add the kale, parsley, rutabaga, sun-dried tomatoes, and carrot and simmer for another 5 minutes, until the carrot is tender.

4. Remove the pot from the heat and squeeze in the lemon juice. Season with salt.

5. Garnish the soup with parsley sprigs and serve hot.

6. Refrigerate leftovers in an airtight container for up to 5 days or freeze for up to 3 months.

Macronutrients: Fat: 59%; Protein: 5%; Carbs: 36%
Per serving: Calories: 56; Total fat: 4g; Total carbs: 6g; Net carbs: 4g; Fiber: 2g; Protein: 1g

# TOM YUM SOUP

› SERVES 8
› DAIRY-FREE, VEGAN

› **PREP TIME:** 10 MINUTES
› **COOK TIME:** 20 MINUTES

This hot and sour soup hailing from Thailand is loaded with low-carb veggies for an easy meal in just 30 minutes. Pre-chop the vegetables the night before to speed up prep time on a busy weeknight. Look for galangal and makrut lime leaves at an Asian market.

8 cups vegetable broth

1-inch knob fresh ginger, peeled and diced

2 garlic cloves, diced

1 teaspoon galangal

2 makrut lime leaves

1 cup coconut cream

1 cup sliced mushrooms

1 cup coarsely chopped broccoli

1 cup coarsely chopped cauliflower

1 Roma tomato, coarsely chopped

½ yellow onion, coarsely chopped

1 cup chopped fresh cilantro

1 lime, cut into 8 wedges

1. In a large stockpot, bring the broth, ginger, garlic, galangal, and lime leaves to a simmer over medium heat.

2. Pour in the coconut cream, followed by the mushrooms, broccoli, cauliflower, tomato, and onion. Simmer for about 15 minutes, until the vegetables are tender.

3. Remove the pot from the heat and serve the soup garnished with the cilantro and a lime wedge.

4. Refrigerate leftovers in an airtight container for up to 5 days or freeze for up to 3 months.

## TIP

For a lighter version of this soup, omit the coconut cream. A good substitute is half an avocado (pureed and stirred into the soup in step 2) to ensure you're getting plenty of healthy fat.

Macronutrients: Fat: 76%; Protein: 6%; Carbs: 18%

Per serving: Calories: 117; Total fat: 11g; Total carbs: 6g; Net carbs: 4g; Fiber: 2g; Protein: 2g

# FRENCH ONION SOUP

› SERVES 8
› DAIRY-FREE, VEGAN

› **PREP TIME:** 10 MINUTES
› **COOK TIME:** 1 HOUR
   20 MINUTES

Traditional French onion soup is made with beef broth, butter, three types of cheese, and crusty French bread to soak up every drop. This vegan version is equally decadent but a lot more nutritious. It's a great choice to serve if you want to impress dinner guests. With the soup casually simmering in the background, your kitchen will smell heavenly.

2 tablespoons avocado or olive oil

3 garlic cloves, chopped

3 thyme sprigs

2 red onions, thinly sliced

1 yellow onion, thinly sliced

1 cup dry marsala

8 cups vegetable broth

Pink Himalayan salt (optional)

1. In a large stockpot, heat the oil over low heat. Add the garlic and thyme and cook for about 1 minute, until the garlic becomes fragrant.

2. Stir in the onions, and caramelize the mixture slowly on low heat, stirring occasionally to prevent the onions from burning, about 20 minutes.

3. Once the onions have taken on a dark brown color, add the marsala, stirring and scraping the bottom of the pan to deglaze it. Add the broth and simmer on low for 1 hour; this will give the soup a wonderfully rich taste. Add extra broth or water if needed. Note that the liquid in the pot will reduce.

4. Remove the pot from the heat and add salt to taste (if using). Serve hot.

5. Refrigerate leftovers in an airtight container for up to 5 days or freeze for up to 3 months.

Macronutrients: Fat: 58%; Protein: 3%; Carbs: 39%

Per serving: Calories: 76; Total fat: 4g; Total carbs: 6g; Net carbs: 5g; Fiber: 1g; Protein: 1g

# EGG ROLL SOUP

› SERVES 6

› **PREP TIME:** 10 MINUTES
› **COOK TIME:** 45 MINUTES

Egg roll in a bowl is a classic keto recipe that everyone seems to know and love. I've taken all those amazing flavors and turned them into an Asian-inspired soup. This brothy soup is loaded with tasty fiber-rich vegetables and a savory broth that's hard to resist.

1 tablespoon salted butter

1 tablespoon sesame oil

½ cup diced yellow onion

8 ounces lean ground pork

2 garlic cloves, minced

1 tablespoon peeled minced ginger

4 cups Chicken Bone Broth (page 26) or store-bought chicken broth

1 (12-to 14-ounce) bag coleslaw shreds

1 tablespoon soy sauce or coconut aminos

½ teaspoon pink Himalayan salt

¼ teaspoon freshly ground black pepper

1 tablespoon sesame seeds

1. In a medium pot, melt the butter over medium heat and add the sesame oil. Add the onion and sauté for about 5 minutes, until softened.

2. Add the pork and, using a wooden spoon or spatula, break up the pork and cook for about 6 minutes until it is no longer pink.

3. Add the garlic and ginger and cook for an additional 2 minutes, until fragrant.

4. Using a large spoon, scoop out the accumulated fat from the pork, leaving about a tablespoon behind for extra flavor and fat.

5. Add the broth to the pot and bring it to a boil. Cover the pot, reduce the heat to low, and simmer for about 20 minutes.

6. Add the coleslaw shreds and bring the soup back to a boil over medium-high heat. Reduce the heat to low and simmer for an additional 5 minutes, or until the coleslaw shreds are tender.

7. Add the soy sauce, salt, and pepper and stir to combine. Divide the soup between bowls and sprinkle with the sesame seeds.

Macronutrients: Fat: 56%; Protein: 31%; Carbs: 14%

Per serving: Calories: 209; Total fat: 13g; Total carbs: 7g; Net carbs: 5g; Fiber: 2g; Protein: 16g

# ROASTED RED PEPPER SOUP

› SERVES 6  › **PREP TIME:** 5 MINUTES
  › **COOK TIME:** 35 MINUTES

Bell peppers are relatively high in carbs, making this soup a bit of a splurge, but it has so much flavor that it's hard to resist. This soup is one of my secret soup recipes. It's so easy to make and the color is so pretty; no one will believe it only took about 30 minutes to cook.

1 tablespoon salted butter

½ cup diced yellow onion

2 garlic cloves, minced

4 red bell peppers, coarsely chopped

4 cups Chicken Bone Broth (page 26) or store-bought chicken broth

2 cups heavy (whipping) cream

½ teaspoon pink Himalayan salt

¼ teaspoon freshly ground black pepper

2 tablespoons sour cream

1 tablespoon water

1. In a medium pot, melt the butter over medium heat. Add the onion and garlic and sauté for about 5 minutes, until softened.

2. Add the bell peppers and cook for an additional 2 to 3 minutes, or until softened.

3. Add the broth and bring to a boil. Then, reduce the heat to low, cover the pot, and simmer for about 15 minutes.

4. Transfer the soup to a blender. With a towel over the lid of the blender and your hand on the lid, pulse the soup in two batches until it is smooth and creamy. (Alternatively, use an immersion blender to puree the soup in the pot.)

5. Return the soup to the pot and stir in the cream. Turn the heat back up to medium to heat the soup through, but don't boil it. Stir in the salt and pepper.

6. Mix the sour cream with the water in a small bowl until it is smooth. Add a dollop or a swirl of the sour cream-water mixture to the top of each bowl as a pretty and tangy garnish.

7. Refrigerate leftovers in an airtight container for up to 3 days or freeze for up to 3 months.

Macronutrients: Fat: 77%; Protein: 12%; Carbs: 11%

Per serving: Calories: 372; Total fat: 32g; Total carbs: 10g; Net carbs: 8g; Fiber: 2g; Protein: 11g

# SPINACH AND ARTICHOKE SOUP

> SERVES 6

> **PREP TIME:** 5 MINUTES
> **COOK TIME:** 40 MINUTES

With bright lemony flavor and oodles of vegetables, this creamy soup tastes a lot like the popular spinach and artichoke dip, but better.

1 tablespoon salted butter

½ cup diced yellow onion

1 garlic clove, minced

4 cups Chicken Bone Broth (page 26) or store-bought chicken broth

1 (14-ounce) can quartered artichoke hearts, drained

½ teaspoon dried thyme

4 ounces fresh baby spinach

2 cups heavy (whipping) cream

1 tablespoon freshly squeezed lemon juice

½ teaspoon pink Himalayan salt

¼ teaspoon freshly ground black pepper

2 tablespoons chopped fresh parsley

6 lemon wedges (optional)

1. In a medium pot, melt the butter over medium heat. Add the onion and garlic and sauté for about 5 minutes, until softened.

2. Add the broth, artichoke hearts, and thyme and bring to a boil. Then, reduce the heat to low, cover the pot, and simmer for about 20 minutes, or until the artichokes are very tender.

3. Add the spinach to the pot and bring the soup back to a boil over medium heat. Reduce the heat to low and simmer for an additional 5 minutes.

4. Transfer the soup to a blender. With a towel over the lid of the blender and your hand on the lid, pulse the soup in two batches until it is smooth and creamy. (Alternatively, use an immersion blender to puree the soup in the pot.)

5. Return the soup to the pot and stir in the cream, then the lemon juice. Turn the heat back up to medium to heat the soup through, but don't boil it.

6. Stir in the salt and pepper and garnish each bowl with 1 teaspoon of the parsley and 1 lemon wedge.

Macronutrients: Fat: 78%; Protein: 12%; Carbs: 10%

Per serving: Calories: 380; Total fat: 32g; Total carbs: 11g; Net carbs: 6g; Fiber: 5g; Protein: 12g

# ITALIAN VEGETABLE SOUP

› SERVES 6

› **PREP TIME:** 10 MINUTES
› **COOK TIME:** 35 MINUTES

If you love vegetables, then this soup is for you. With a rich and savory broth and loads of tender veggies, you can fill up on flavor and fiber with this keto-friendly soup.

2 tablespoons salted butter
½ cup diced yellow onion
½ cup diced celery
½ cup sliced carrots
1 garlic clove, minced

4 cups Beef Bone Broth (page 27) or store-bought beef broth
1 (14-ounce) can diced tomatoes
8 ounces green beans, trimmed and cut into ½-inch pieces

1 tablespoon Italian seasoning
1 cup diced zucchini
1 teaspoon pink Himalayan salt
¼ teaspoon freshly ground black pepper

1. In a medium pot, melt the butter over low heat. Add the onion, celery, carrots, and garlic. Sauté until the onions are soft, about 5 minutes.

2. Add the broth, tomatoes and their juices, green beans, and Italian seasoning and bring to a boil. Cover the pot, reduce the heat to low, and simmer for 20 minutes.

3. Add the zucchini, then increase the heat to medium to bring the soup back to a boil. Reduce the heat to low and simmer for an additional 2 minutes to cook the zucchini.

4. Stir in the salt and pepper and serve.

5. Refrigerate leftovers in an airtight container for up to 3 days or freeze for up to 3 months.

## TIP

Replace the beef broth with vegetable broth to make this recipe vegetarian. Feel free to add more vegetables, too, such as shredded cabbage, eggplant, a handful of peas (unless you're doing strict keto), and even spinach or Swiss chard.

Macronutrients: Fat: 33%; Protein: 37%; Carbs: 30%

Per serving: Calories: 108; Total fat: 4g; Total carbs: 8g; Net carbs: 5g; Fiber: 3g; Protein: 10g

# HERB AND OLIVE
# FOCACCIA

Page 106

# 6

# Breads, Crackers, and Toppings

# SESAME SEED CRACKERS

› MAKES 20 CRACKERS

› **PREP TIME:** 15 MINUTES
› **COOK TIME:** 50 MINUTES
  TO 1 HOUR

Deliciously crispy, these sesame seed crackers are packed with spices and cheesy flavor. The dough for these crackers is straightforward and comes together quickly. Then it's just a matter of rolling the dough thinly between parchment paper, slicing, and baking. These crackers can be enjoyed as is or served alongside Tom Yum Soup (page 92) or Egg Roll Soup (page 94).

½ cup shredded sharp cheddar cheese

½ cup finely grated shelf-stable Parmesan cheese

½ cup grated Parmesan cheese

½ cup coconut flour

½ cup sesame seeds

2 teaspoons psyllium husk powder

1 teaspoon baking powder

1 teaspoon onion powder

1 teaspoon garlic powder

1 teaspoon dried basil

1 teaspoon dried oregano

½ teaspoon sea salt

¼ teaspoon freshly ground black pepper

¼ teaspoon red pepper flakes

1 cup water

3 tablespoons avocado oil or extra-virgin olive oil

1 large egg, at room temperature

2 tablespoons white sesame seeds

2 tablespoons black sesame seeds

1. Preheat the oven to 350°F. Line a large baking sheet with parchment paper and set aside.

2. In a large mixing bowl, combine the cheddar cheese, Parmesan, coconut flour, sesame seeds, psyllium husk powder, baking powder, onion powder, garlic powder, basil, oregano, salt, pepper, and red pepper flakes. Stir until well combined. Add the water, oil, and egg and stir until a smooth dough forms.

3. Divide the dough in half and roll one half out thinly between 2 sheets of parchment paper. The thinner you roll out the dough, the crispier the crackers will be.

4. Using a pizza cutter, cut the dough into 10 equal pieces, and carefully place them on a baking sheet lined with parchment paper. (You may need to transfer them with a pancake spatula.) Sprinkle the white and black sesame seeds on top of the crackers.

5. Bake for 25 to 30 minutes, or until lightly browned around the edges. Repeat with the other half of the dough.

6. Allow the crackers to cool fully on the baking sheet before serving.

7. Refrigerate leftovers in an airtight container for up to 5 days or freeze for up to 3 weeks.

## TIP

You can opt for a more organic shape and bake the whole cracker dough on 2 baking sheets. Once they are baked and cooled, you can break them into pieces.

Macronutrients: Fat: 77%; Protein: 15%; Carbs: 8%
Per serving: Calories: 96; Total fat: 9g; Total carbs: 3g; Net carbs: 2g; Fiber: 1g; Protein: 4g

# ROSEMARY FLATBREAD

> ‣ MAKES 6 FLATBREADS
> ‣ DAIRY-FREE, VEGETARIAN

> ‣ **PREP TIME:** 10 MINUTES
> ‣ **COOK TIME:** 25 TO 35 MINUTES

The basis of any great flatbread is the dough, and this rosemary-infused flatbread works beautifully despite the lack of gluten. With just a few key ingredients, you can enjoy a perfect keto option that can be served as an appetizer or alongside a keto meal. The best part is that this recipe comes together quickly, allowing you to enjoy it fast and often.

1½ tablespoons golden flax meal

1½ cups finely milled almond flour, sifted

2 teaspoons psyllium husk powder

1 teaspoon baking powder

¼ teaspoon xanthan gum

¼ teaspoon sea salt

¼ teaspoon onion powder

¼ teaspoon garlic powder

½ cup hot water

1 large egg, at room temperature

1 tablespoon extra-virgin olive oil, plus more for brushing

1½ tablespoons chopped fresh rosemary

Sea salt flakes, for topping

1. Preheat the oven to 400°F. Line a large baking sheet with a silicone baking mat or parchment paper and set aside.

2. In a coffee grinder, grind the flax meal until it's a fine powder. In a large bowl, combine the flax meal powder, almond flour, psyllium husk powder, baking powder, xanthan gum, sea salt, onion powder, and garlic powder. Add the hot water, egg, and oil. Mix the dough well with a silicone spatula.

3. Scoop 6 equal portions of the dough onto the baking sheet. With wet hands, form the dough into circles. Be sure to keep your hands wet, because the dough will be very sticky.

4. Use a pastry brush to brush each flatbread with oil. Sprinkle the tops evenly with the rosemary and sea salt flakes. Bake for 25 to 35 minutes, or until lightly browned.

5. Serve this flatbread straight from the oven. Cooling is not necessary.

6. Store leftovers in an airtight container at room temperature for 1 to 2 days, refrigerate for up to 5 days, or freeze for up to 3 weeks.

Macronutrients: Fat: 73%; Protein: 13%; Carbs: 14%

Per serving: Calories: 181; Total fat: 16g; Total carbs: 6g; Net carbs: 2g; Fiber: 4g; Protein: 6g

# BUTTERMILK BISCUITS

› MAKES 10 BISCUITS
› VEGETARIAN

› **PREP TIME:** 10 MINUTES
› **COOK TIME:** 20 MINUTES

Now you can enjoy the tangy flavor of buttermilk biscuits without the high carbs of traditional biscuits. This recipe is tender and flaky and has a distinct buttermilk flavor without using any milk. The secret is a combination of sour cream, melted butter, and apple cider vinegar. These biscuits are sure to satisfy your craving for bread and butter with your hearty bowl of soup while keeping you in ketosis.

1¾ cups finely milled almond flour

2 tablespoons coconut flour

1 tablespoon baking powder

¼ teaspoon sea salt

½ cup sour cream

6 tablespoons (¾ stick) unsalted butter, melted, divided

1 teaspoon apple cider vinegar

2 large eggs, at room temperature

1. Preheat the oven to 375°F. Line a large baking sheet with a silicone baking mat or parchment paper and set aside.

2. In a large bowl, sift together the almond flour, coconut flour, baking powder, and salt. Add the sour cream, 4 tablespoons of melted butter, the apple cider vinegar, and the eggs. Use a fork to mix until fully combined.

3. Drop the dough in 10 large spoonfuls onto the baking sheet and brush the tops of each biscuit with the remaining 2 tablespoons of melted butter. Bake the biscuits for 20 minutes, or until lightly golden brown on top.

4. Serve hot or warm.

5. Refrigerate leftovers in an airtight container for up to 5 days or freeze for up to 3 weeks.

Macronutrients: Fat: 81%; Protein: 10%; Carbs: 9%
Per serving: Calories: 199; Total fat: 19g; Total carbs: 5g; Net carbs: 3g; Fiber: 2g; Protein: 5g

# CHEDDAR-CHIVE BISCUITS

› MAKES 10 BISCUITS

› **PREP TIME:** 10 MINUTES
› **COOK TIME:** 20 MINUTES

One bite of these melt-in-your-mouth biscuits will have you convinced that this keto diet thing can indeed be delicious. The recipe uses a combination of almond flour, coconut flour, and sour cream to produce the perfect fluffy, low-carb biscuits. Why crave a traditional biscuit when you can have a tender keto one in about half an hour?

1¾ cup finely milled almond flour

2 tablespoons coconut flour

1 tablespoon baking powder

¼ teaspoon sea salt

½ cup sour cream

½ cup shredded sharp cheddar cheese

4 tablespoons (½ stick) unsalted butter, melted, plus more for serving

2 large eggs, at room temperature

2 tablespoons finely chopped chives

2 tablespoons grated Parmesan cheese

1. Preheat the oven to 375°F. Line a large baking sheet with a silicone baking mat or parchment paper and set aside.

2. In a large bowl, sift together the almond flour, coconut flour, baking powder, and salt. Add the sour cream, cheddar cheese, melted butter, eggs, and chives. Use a fork to mix until fully combined.

3. Drop the dough in 10 large spoonfuls onto the baking sheet and sprinkle the top of each biscuit with the Parmesan. Bake the biscuits for 20 minutes, or until lightly golden brown on top.

4. Serve your biscuits hot from the oven with butter.

5. Refrigerate leftovers in an airtight container for up to 5 days or freeze for up to 3 weeks.

Macronutrients: Fat: 78%; Protein: 12%; Carbs: 10%

Per serving: Calories: 206; Total fat: 19g; Total carbs: 5g; Net carbs: 3g; Fiber: 2g; Protein: 7g

# CHEESY GARLIC ROLLS

› MAKES 12 ROLLS

› **PREP TIME:** 10 MINUTES

› **COOK TIME:** 25 TO 30 MINUTES

There is nothing like the smell of freshly baked cheesy garlic rolls to bring the family running to the kitchen. With just a few key ingredients, you can make a keto-friendly side dish that you can gladly say yes to.

1½ cups shredded mozzarella cheese

¼ cup cream cheese, at room temperature

2 large eggs, at room temperature

¾ cup finely milled almond flour, sifted

3 tablespoons unsalted butter, melted

1 teaspoon extra-virgin olive oil

2 garlic cloves, minced

¼ teaspoon garlic salt

¼ cup grated Parmesan cheese

¼ cup chopped fresh flat-leaf parsley

1. Preheat the oven to 350°F. Line a large baking sheet with parchment paper and set aside.

2. Place the mozzarella cheese in a medium microwave-safe bowl. Microwave in 30-second increments, making sure to stir each time, until fully melted. Add the cream cheese and combine well. Allow the mixture to cool slightly, then stir in the eggs and almond flour. The dough will be sticky.

3. Using wet hands, separate the dough into 12 equal parts, shape into rounds, and place on the prepared baking sheet.

4. To make the garlic butter, in a small bowl, combine the butter, oil, garlic, and garlic salt. With a pastry brush, spread the garlic butter on top of each roll and sprinkle with the Parmesan.

5. Bake for 25 to 30 minutes, until lightly golden. Top with the parsley right out of the oven. Serve hot or warm.

6. Refrigerate leftovers in an airtight container for up to 3 days.

Macronutrients: Fat: 75%; Protein: 18%; Carbs: 7%

Per serving: Calories: 144; Total fat: 12g; Total carbs: 2g; Net carbs: 1g; Fiber: 1g; Protein: 6g

# HERB AND OLIVE FOCACCIA

› MAKES 10 SQUARES
› VEGETARIAN

› **PREP TIME:** 10 MINUTES
› **COOK TIME:** 25 TO
   35 MINUTES

You can enjoy your favorite part of Italian restaurants and stay within your macros. This focaccia comes together so quickly and easily that it will become a staple in your home in no time. Pair it with Tuscan Meatball Soup (page 34) or Italian Wedding Soup (page 54).

**For the bread**

3 tablespoons golden flax meal

3 cups finely milled almond flour, sifted

1 tablespoon psyllium husk powder

2 teaspoons baking powder

½ teaspoon xanthan gum

½ teaspoon sea salt

½ teaspoon onion powder

½ teaspoon garlic powder

1 cup hot water

3 tablespoons extra-virgin olive oil, divided

2 large eggs, at room temperature

20 kalamata olives, pitted

2 teaspoons sea salt flakes

¼ teaspoon red pepper flakes

**For the dipping oil**

½ cup extra-virgin olive oil

1 tablespoon sea salt

1 tablespoon dried oregano

1 tablespoon dried rosemary

2 teaspoons freshly ground black pepper

2 teaspoons red pepper flakes

**To make the bread**

1. Preheat the oven to 400°F. Line a large baking sheet with a silicone baking mat or parchment paper and set aside.

2. In a coffee grinder, grind the flax meal until it's a fine powder. In a large bowl, combine the flax meal powder, almond flour, psyllium husk powder, baking powder, xanthan gum, sea salt, onion powder, and garlic powder. Add the hot water, 1 tablespoon of olive oil, and the eggs. Mix the dough well with a silicone spatula.

3. With wet hands, spread the dough evenly over the baking sheet. Using a pastry brush, spread the remaining 2 tablespoons of olive oil over the entire surface of the dough. Sprinkle the olives, sea salt flakes, and red pepper flakes over the top. Lightly press the olives into the dough.

4. Bake for 25 to 35 minutes, or until lightly browned.

**To make the dipping oil and finish the bread**

5. While the bread is baking, in a small bowl, combine the olive oil, salt, oregano, rosemary, pepper, and red pepper flakes.

6. Remove the bread from the oven and cut it into 10 squares. Enjoy while still warm with the dipping oil.

7. Refrigerate leftover bread for up to 5 days or freeze for up to 3 weeks. Store any leftover dipping oil in an airtight container in a cool, dry place for 7 to 10 days.

## TIP

You can customize this focaccia any way you like by substituting your favorite toppings, herbs, and spices. For example, instead of olives, you could use halved cherry tomatoes for a roasted tomato and herb focaccia if that fits with your macros.

Macronutrients: Fat: 82%; Protein: 8%; Carbs: 10%
Per serving: Calories: 333; Total fat: 32g; Total carbs: 8g; Net carbs: 3g; Fiber: 5g; Protein: 8g

# ONION-CHEDDAR BREAD

> SERVES 12
> VEGETARIAN

> **PREP TIME:** 15 MINUTES
> **COOK TIME:** 45 TO
> 55 MINUTES, PLUS
> 1 HOUR TO COOL

This savory keto bread pays homage to the South's prized Vidalia onion. Sweet, caramelized onion pairs perfectly with sharp cheddar in this loaf to make a bread that's perfect for eating alongside, or dipping in, any bowl of soup or stew. Serve with Watercress-Spinach Soup (page 90) or Cream of Asparagus Soup (page 72).

2 tablespoons unsalted butter, plus more for preparing the pan

½ cup chopped Vidalia onion

8 large eggs

1 cup almond flour

½ cup coconut flour

2 teaspoons baking powder

1 teaspoon baking soda

½ teaspoon kosher salt

¼ teaspoon onion powder

¼ teaspoon garlic powder

¼ teaspoon freshly ground black pepper

⅛ teaspoon ground cayenne pepper

5 tablespoons unsalted butter, melted

2 tablespoons sour cream

1 cup shredded sharp cheddar cheese

1. Preheat the oven to 350°F. Coat an 8-by-4-inch loaf pan with butter and line it with parchment paper overhanging two sides. Set aside.

2. In a small sauté pan or skillet, melt 2 tablespoons butter over medium heat. Add the onion and sauté for 7 to 10 minutes until the onion is translucent and begins to caramelize.

3. In the bowl of a stand mixer fitted with the whisk attachment, or in a large bowl with an electric hand mixer, whip the eggs for about 2 minutes, until light and foamy. Add the almond and coconut flours, baking powder, baking soda, salt, onion powder, garlic powder, black pepper, and cayenne. Mix on medium speed until combined, scraping down the sides at least once.

4. Add the melted butter and sour cream and mix well to combine. Stir in the cheddar cheese and cooked onion.

5. Spoon the batter into the prepared loaf pan and smooth the top. Bake for 45 to 55 minutes, or until a tester inserted into the center comes out clean.

6. Let cool in the pan for 30 minutes. Lifting by the parchment paper, transfer the loaf to a wire rack to cool for another 30 minutes before serving.

7. Refrigerate leftovers tightly wrapped for 3 to 4 days or freeze for up to 3 months.

**TIP**

For onion-cheddar grilled cheese dippers, preheat a small skillet over medium heat. Take two ½-inch-thick slices of onion-cheddar bread and sandwich one slice of Colby cheese between them. Butter both sides of the sandwich and place it in the hot skillet. Cook for 2 to 3 minutes on each side, until golden and toasty. Cut the sandwich into three pieces and serve with a warm bowl of soup.

Macronutrients: Fat: 77%; Protein: 16%; Carbs: 7%
Per serving: Calories: 210; Total fat: 19g; Total carbs: 4g; Net carbs: 3g; Fiber: 1g; Protein: 8g

# JALAPEÑO-CHEESE BREAD

› MAKES 12 SLICES

› **PREP TIME:** 10 MINUTES
› **COOK TIME:** 50 MINUTES
  TO 1 HOUR, PLUS
  45 MINUTES TO COOL

With just a few essential ingredients from your keto pantry, you can make a yummy, low-carb baked bread loaded with cheesy jalapeño goodness. Your taste buds and sugar levels will thank you for adding this classic flavor combination in keto-friendly form. Toast this bread to use in a sandwich or eat it as is. No matter how you slice it, this bread is made for eating.

4 tablespoons (½ stick) unsalted butter, melted, plus more to grease the pan

1 cup golden flax meal

¾ cup coconut flour

2 tablespoons granulated erythritol–monk fruit blend

3 tablespoons grated Parmesan cheese

1 tablespoon psyllium husk powder

2 teaspoons baking powder

1 teaspoon sea salt

¼ teaspoon freshly ground black pepper

8 ounces cream cheese, at room temperature

4 large eggs, at room temperature

3 cups shredded sharp cheddar cheese, divided

⅓ cup pickled jalapeño peppers, drained and diced

1¼ cups full-fat unsweetened coconut milk or almond milk

1. Preheat the oven to 375°F. Grease a 9-by-5-inch loaf pan with butter and line it with parchment paper overhanging two sides. Set aside.

2. In a coffee grinder, grind the flax meal until it's a fine powder. In a large bowl, combine the flax meal powder, coconut flour, erythritol–monk fruit blend, Parmesan, psyllium husk powder, baking powder, salt, and pepper. Set aside.

3. In another large bowl, using an electric mixer on high speed, combine the cream cheese and eggs. Add 2 cups of cheddar cheese and the pickled jalapeño peppers. Stir until well incorporated.

4. Add the dry ingredients to the wet ingredients and combine well. Using a rubber spatula, fold in the melted butter. Add the coconut milk and mix until just combined. The batter will be thick.

5. Spread the batter in the prepared loaf pan. Top with the remaining 1 cup of cheddar cheese. Bake for 50 minutes to 1 hour, until the top is lightly browned and a toothpick inserted into the center comes out clean. Check the bread at the 45-minute mark, cover the top with aluminum foil to ensure it doesn't burn, and continue to bake until fully done.

6. Remove the bread from the oven and place it on a wire rack. Allow to cool for at least 15 minutes in the pan. Using the parchment paper to lift, remove the loaf from the pan and cool for another 30 minutes on a wire rack before slicing.

7. Refrigerate leftovers in an airtight container for up to 5 days or freeze for up to 3 weeks.

## TIP

Serve with Jambalaya Soup (page 51) or Chicken and Cauli Rice Soup (page 52).

Macronutrients: Fat: 79%; Protein: 14%; Carbs: 7%
Per serving: Calories: 358; Total fat: 32g; Total carbs: 6g; Net carbs: 3g; Fiber: 3g; Protein: 13g;
Erythritol: 2g

# MEASUREMENT CONVERSIONS

| | US STANDARD | US STANDARD (OUNCES) | METRIC (APPROXIMATE) |
|---|---|---|---|
| **VOLUME EQUIVALENTS (LIQUID)** | 2 TABLESPOONS | 1 FL. OZ. | 30 ML |
| | ¼ CUP | 2 FL. OZ. | 60 ML |
| | ½ CUP | 4 FL. OZ. | 120 ML |
| | 1 CUP | 8 FL. OZ. | 240 ML |
| | 1½ CUPS | 12 FL. OZ. | 355 ML |
| | 2 CUPS OR 1 PINT | 16 FL. OZ. | 475 ML |
| | 4 CUPS OR 1 QUART | 32 FL. OZ. | 1 L |
| | 1 GALLON | 128 FL. OZ. | 4 L |
| **VOLUME EQUIVALENTS (DRY)** | ⅛ TEASPOON | | 0.5 ML |
| | ¼ TEASPOON | | 1 ML |
| | ½ TEASPOON | | 2 ML |
| | ¾ TEASPOON | | 4 ML |
| | 1 TEASPOON | | 5 ML |
| | 1 TABLESPOON | | 15 ML |
| | ¼ CUP | | 59 ML |
| | ⅓ CUP | | 79 ML |
| | ½ CUP | | 118 ML |
| | ⅔ CUP | | 156 ML |
| | ¾ CUP | | 177 ML |
| | 1 CUP | | 235 ML |
| | 2 CUPS OR 1 PINT | | 475 ML |
| | 3 CUPS | | 700 ML |
| | 4 CUPS OR 1 QUART | | 1 L |
| | ½ GALLON | | 2 L |
| | 1 GALLON | | 4 L |
| **WEIGHT EQUIVALENTS** | ½ OUNCE | | 15 G |
| | 1 OUNCE | | 30 G |
| | 2 OUNCES | | 60 G |
| | 4 OUNCES | | 115 G |
| | 8 OUNCES | | 225 G |
| | 12 OUNCES | | 340 G |
| | 16 OUNCES OR 1 POUND | | 455 G |

# INDEX

# ACKNOWLEDGMENTS

I'd like to thank my husband, Matthew, for helping me reach so many new heights (and not just metaphorically—I'm short, and he's tall), and I wouldn't have the confidence to pursue my passions without his support. Also, thank you to my son, Kegan. I'd never have become a successful blogger and recipe developer without him. He's my tech team, videographer, and extra pair of hands, and he has even coded a few things for the website. You're so awesome—you can live in the basement forever! Brenna, your unwavering support means the world to me, and you are hands-down the best recipe tester on the planet. Your enthusiasm is infectious, lifting me up whenever going on seems so hard. Also, a huge shout-out to my girls, Robin, Wendy, Brianne, Renee, and Kat: You're all so supportive and amazing. I wouldn't be here without you. Finally, much thanks and appreciation to Rachelle Mahoney, a fantastic editor without whom this book would never exist.

# ABOUT THE AUTHOR

**Jennifer Allen** is a retired professional chef with several successful businesses behind her. Living in Texas for more than 20 years has inspired her recipe creation, with lively Southwestern flavors popping up in many of her recipes. She's now cooking north of the border in Ontario, Canada, where she lives with her family and four-legged best friend and the cats who rule them all. She continues to post her recipes at KetoCookingWins.com and creates non-keto recipes for the rest of the family. The recipes can be found at CookWhatYouLove.com.